Historical Atlas of Canada

Third Revised Edition

D.G.G. Kerr

Department of History,
University of Western Ontario

Nelson

© Thomas Nelson & Sons (Canada) Limited
1961, 1966, 1975
81 Curlew Drive
Don Mills, Ontario
M3A 2R1

First published 1961. Second edition, 1966.
Revised third edition, 1975

ISBN 0-176-00409-2

Printed and bound in Canada

Acknowledgements

The publishers wish to acknowledge with thanks the co-operation of members of the Canadian Historical Association who checked map proofs, and the valuable assistance given by the Public Archives, Ottawa, and Statistics Canada. We also thank the Canadian Railroad Historical Association of Montreal for helpful information concerning the various railway maps.

Cartography: Preparation by C. C. J. Bond, drawing by Ellsworth Walsh, Edward Banks, Roy Petticrew, and David L. Fryer. Map 3 from Leverett and Taylor, in Atwood's *Physiographic Provinces of North America* (Ginn and Company, Toronto).

Ship drawings: John R. Stevens, Maritime Museum of Canada

Other drawings: Roy Petticrew

Revised Third Edition
Pages 1–85, 97–101, research by Dr. Leonard Guelke and Fiona Cowles of Map Research and Design Limited, design by Paul Kaufhold, execution by David L. Fryer & Co. Pages 86–96, research by Mary Robson, design by Paul Kaufhold, drawing by Dan Giangualano.

Publishers' Preface

First published in 1961, with the encourage ment and advice of the Canadian Historic Association, the *Historical Atlas of Cana* has since occupied a unique and invaluab position in libraries and classrooms. The co sistent demand for this book has been amp proof that such an atlas is integral in ar thorough study of Canadian history. Historic events and trends can often be clearly unde stood only if examined in terms of Canada geographical environment. This is especial evident in the study of topics such as explora tion, settlement, development of trade ar transportation, drawing of boundary line and waging of wars.

Since the last revision, much has occurre that has pointed to the necessity for furthe editing and updating. Hence this new ar greatly improved edition. The main change are these:

● Additional statistical material has bee introduced. Part Six now covers a broad spectrum of Canada's economic, political ar social life from 1871 to the most recent censu The data is presented graphically in a conci new form so that the user can easily obta whatever information is required.

● Part Five has been revised to accor modate recent developments.

● The Atlas has been completely metr cated.

● The bibliography has been updated t include recent titles.

Contents

iii

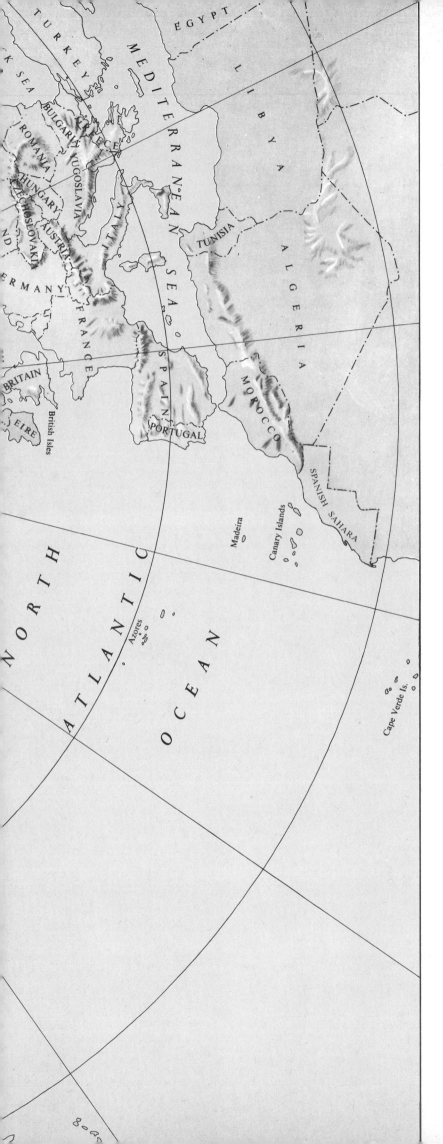

PART ONE

ENVIRONMENT AND

PREHISTORY

1   Canada and her Environment

Canada lay undiscovered, beyond the bounds of the known world, until recent centuries. Her history gradually began as she became part of a North Atlantic community centred in western Europe, a community to which Canada supplied fish and furs and later other products of her forests, fields, and mountains. The North Atlantic remained an area of vital importance to Canada even in the nineteenth century and afterwards, when transcontinental expansion made her more solidly North American and gave her an outlook on the Pacific as well. Most recently, a tilting world perspective has revealed a new neighbour across the North Pole.

2 The Ice Ages

The North American continent was gradually formed during millions of years by great upheavals and other changes in the earth's crust. In the most recent or Pleistocene geologic age (beginning about a million years

3 The Retreating Ice

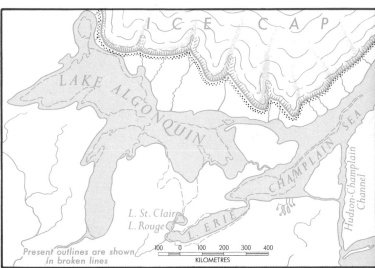

Present outlines are shown in broken lines

KILOMETRES

ago) there were successive Ice Ages during which huge glaciers carried with them into what is now the United States much of the surface of the Canadian Shield. At the same time they gouged out large troughs which some thirty thousand years ago when the ice finally melted, became lakes and rivers—the canoe highways of the early explorers and traders. Later Canadian history, including for example the location of the Great Lakes and St. Lawrence section of the boundary with the United States, was also largely influenced by the movement of Pleistocene ice.

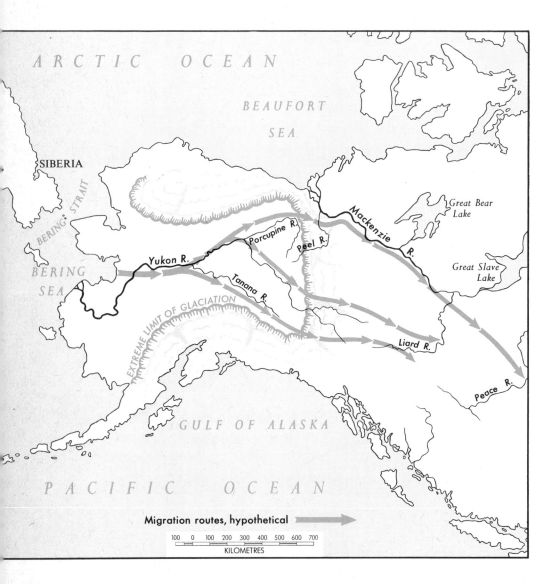

Migration routes, hypothetical

KILOMETRES

4 The Indian and Eskimo Entry

It has long been thought likely that the Indians and Eskimos entered North America by the easy passage from Siberia across the Bering Strait at the time when the retreating ice left a way open on the eastern slope of the Rockies between the Cordilleran and Keewatin Ice Caps. Archaeological investigation, still in its early stages, has strengthened this belief by the discovery of primitive stone implements and other remains at several points along probable routes.

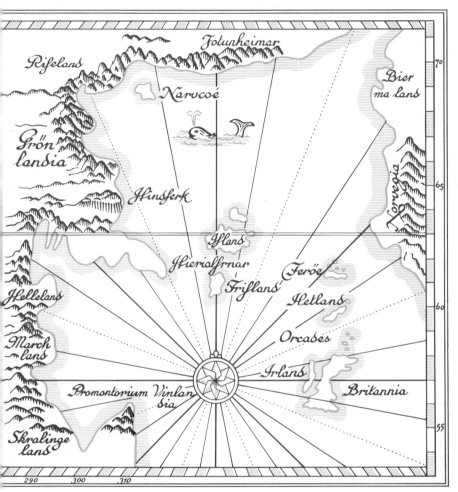

5 The Vikings in North America

References in Norse sagas show that the Vikings reached North America in the tenth or eleventh century. Their discoveries, almost unknown to the rest of Europe, seem to have had little or no influence on subsequent European or American history. Much controversy has resulted from attempts to locate such regions as Markland and Vinland, and from claims regarding the discovery of supposedly Viking relics at various places in North America. In fact, however, our certain knowledge of the Vikings in America is little clearer than that of the Icelander, Sigurdus Stephanius, whose map of 1570 is reproduced here.

6 The World of Martin Behaim, 1492

Behaim, a young German who had spent some time in Portugal, constructed in Nuremberg in 1492 a terrestrial globe. Its western hemisphere, shown here, makes clear that, although his view of the world was less accurate than that of the best geographers of his time, it was very similar to that on which Columbus based his journey westward that same year. There is no evidence that the two men may have met.

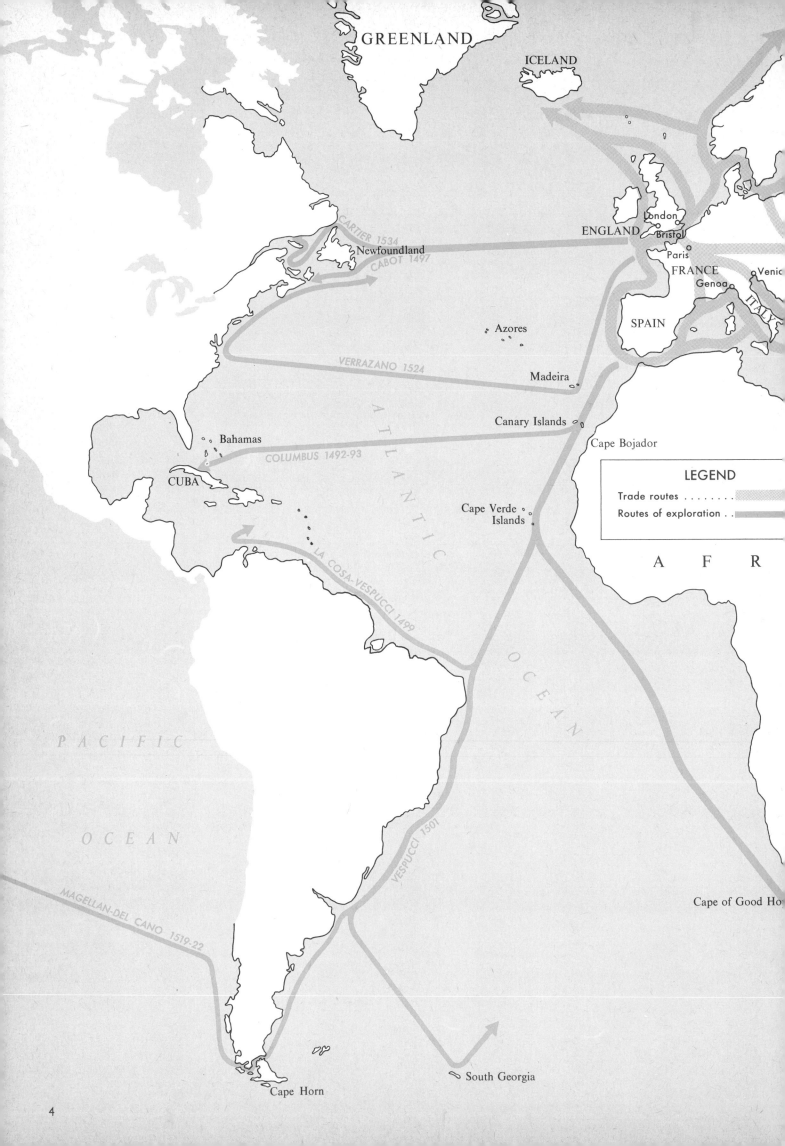

GREENLAND

ICELAND

CARTIER 1534

Newfoundland

CABOT 1497

ENGLAND

London
Bristol

Paris

FRANCE

Venic

Genoa

ITALY

SPAIN

Azores

VERRAZANO 1524

Madeira

Canary Islands

Cape Bojador

Bahamas

COLUMBUS 1492-93

CUBA

A T L A N T I C

LEGEND

Trade routes . . . .

Routes of exploration . . .

A F R

Cape Verde
Islands

LA COSA-VESPUCCI 1499

O C E A N

P A C I F I C

O C E A N

VESPUCCI 1501

MAGELLAN-DEL CANO 1519-22

Cape of Good Ho

South Georgia

Cape Horn

4

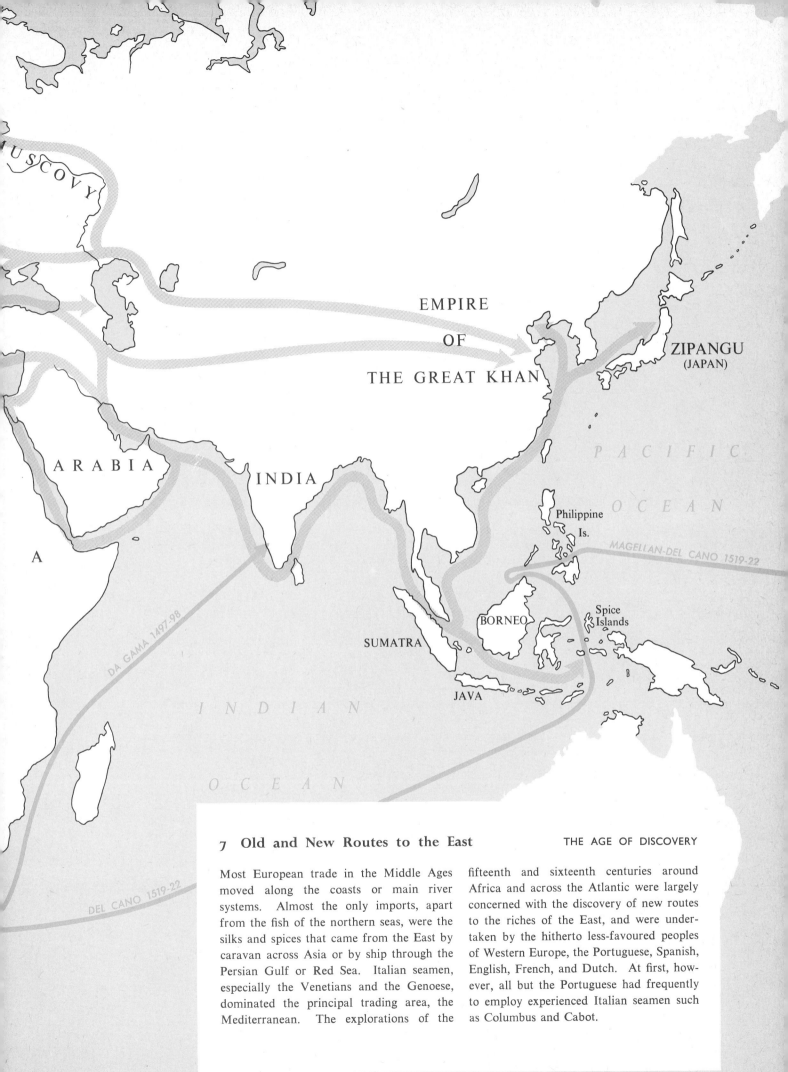

MUSCOVY

EMPIRE

OF

THE GREAT KHAN

ZIPANGU
(JAPAN)

ARABIA

INDIA

A

PACIFIC

OCEAN

Philippine
Is.

MAGELLAN-DEL CANO 1519-22

DA GAMA 1497-98

BORNEO

Spice
Islands

SUMATRA

JAVA

INDIAN

OCEAN

DEL CANO 1519-22

7 Old and New Routes to the East

THE AGE OF DISCOVERY

Most European trade in the Middle Ages moved along the coasts or main river systems. Almost the only imports, apart from the fish of the northern seas, were the silks and spices that came from the East by caravan across Asia or by ship through the Persian Gulf or Red Sea. Italian seamen, especially the Venetians and the Genoese, dominated the principal trading area, the Mediterranean. The explorations of the fifteenth and sixteenth centuries around Africa and across the Atlantic were largely concerned with the discovery of new routes to the riches of the East, and were undertaken by the hitherto less-favoured peoples of Western Europe, the Portuguese, Spanish, English, French, and Dutch. At first, however, all but the Portuguese had frequently to employ experienced Italian seamen such as Columbus and Cabot.

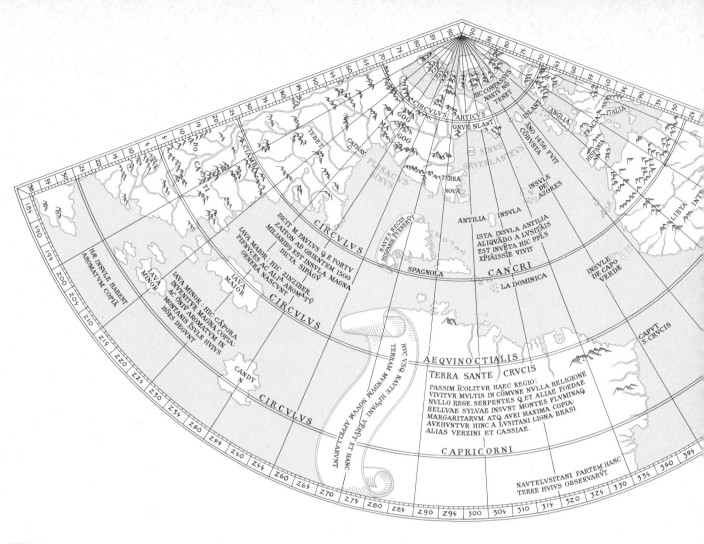

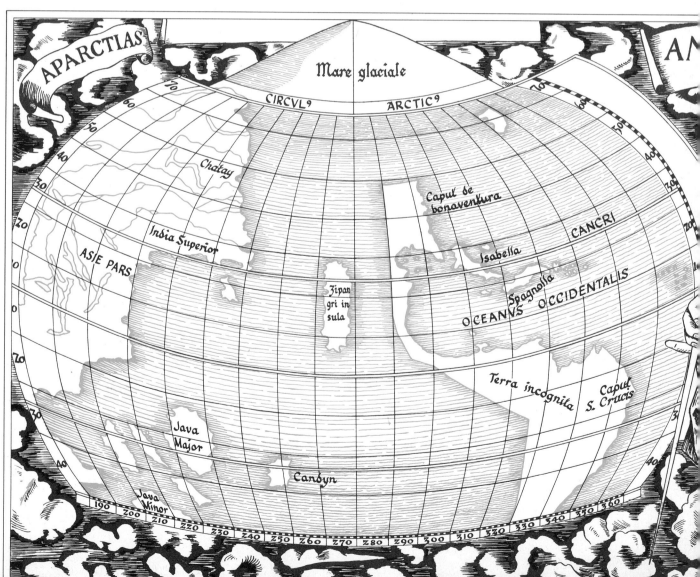

8 Part of Ruysch's Map, 1507

First Impressions of America

When Columbus died in 1506, the significance of his discoveries was still obscure. His own belief and that of many others that Asia and its adjacent islands had been reached is illustrated in the Johannes Ruysch map of 1507. As early as 1502, however, Amerigo Vespucci, another traveller in the New World, had expressed the opinion that this was a separate continent. Martin Waldseemüller's map, published in the same year as that of Ruysch, is the first to be based on Vespucci's theory and the first to apply, in the latter's honour, the name 'America' to the new continent.

9 Part of Waldseemüller's Map, 1507

10 The name 'America' appears on a map for the first time

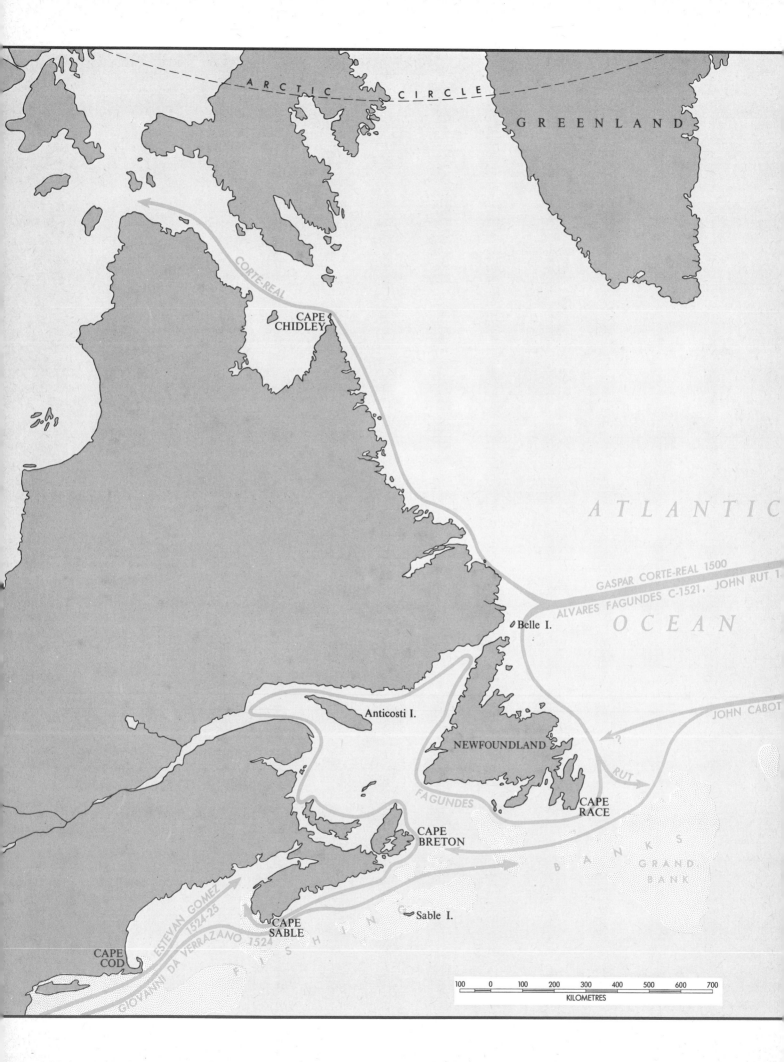

ARCTIC CIRCLE

GREENLAND

CORTE-REAL

CAPE
CHIDLEY

A T L A N T I C

GASPAR CORTE-REAL 1500

ALVARES FAGUNDES C-1521, JOHN RUT 1.

O C E A N

Belle I.

Anticosti I.

JOHN CABOT

NEWFOUNDLAND

?

RUT

FAGUNDES

CAPE
RACE

CAPE
BRETON

B A N K S

GRAND
BANK

ESTEVAN GOMEZ 1524-25

Sable I.

F I S H I N G

CAPE
SABLE

CAPE
COD

GIOVANNI DA VERRAZANO 1524

| 100 | 0 | 100 | 200 | 300 | 400 | 500 | 600 | 700 |

KILOMETRES

11 Exploration of the North-east Coastline

Records of how the coastline from the Bay of Fundy to Hudson Bay was explored are meagre, and their interpretation has caused much controversy. Expeditions were officially authorized by no less than four governments. Sailing under the English flag were the Genoese John Cabot, his son Sebastian (whose story is especially controversial), and the Englishman John Rut. Gaspar Corte-Real, his brother Miguel, and Alvarez Fagundes served their native Portugal. Giovanni da Verrazano was a Florentine employed by the King of France and Estevan Gomez a Portuguese employed by Spain. There were others as well, and some no doubt about whom no record remains. After the earliest voyages, hope of other Mexicos or Perus rich in gold and silver waned, and the primary objective became to find a way through or north of what seemed an unfortunate obstacle on the route to Asia. Meanwhile, however, the major discovery actually made, the great fishing banks, began immediately to attract increasing numbers of fishermen from England, France, and Portugal.

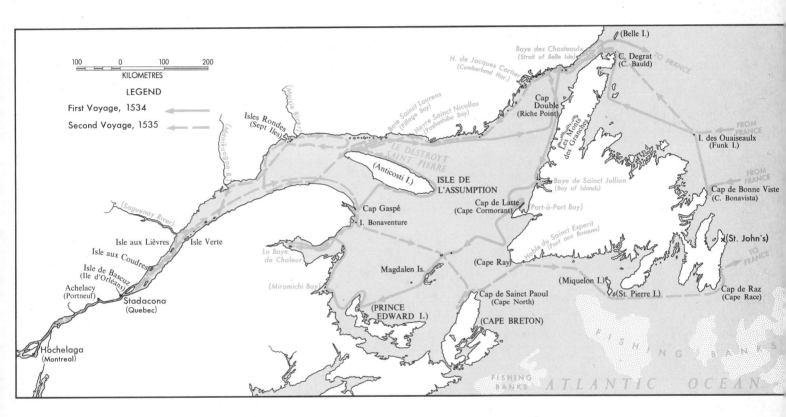

12 The Voyages of Jacques Cartier

The first explorer known to have penetrated much beyond the coastline into what is now Canada was Jacques Cartier. Supported by Francis I of France, Cartier spent the summer of 1534 exploring the Gulf of St. Lawrence, and the following year ascended the St. Lawrence River as far as the Indian villages of Stadacona (Quebec) and Hochelaga (Montreal). After glimpsing the upper reaches of the St. Lawrence and learning of the Ottawa as well, he returned to Stadacona for the winter and thence to France. By this time earlier hopes for a passage through to the Pacific had dimmed, but Indian tales, especially of the Kingdom of the Saguenay, convinced Cartier and Francis I that a rich territory, perhaps in north-eastern Asia, was not much farther up river. Delayed until 1541 by events in Europe, a major expedition under a courtier, the Sieur de Roberval, as military commander and Cartier as chief pilot was sent to establish a colony in Canada as a base for the conquest of the Saguenay. Failure, partly due to quarrelling and bad luck, but inevitable because of the nature of the objective, was followed by a long lull in official French interest in the region.

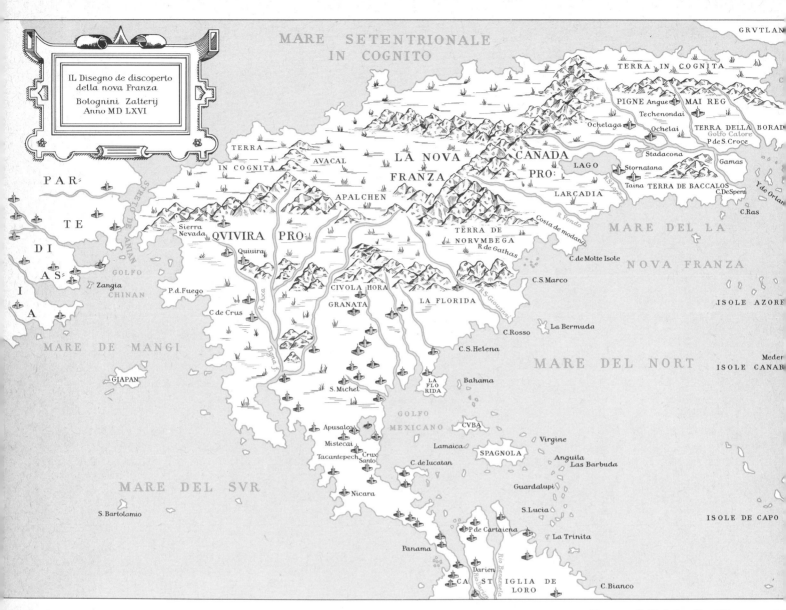

The map contains the following labels:

GRVTLAN

MARE SETENTRIONALE
IN COGNITO

TERRA IN COGNITA

PIGNE Angue MAI REG
Techenondai
Ochelaga   Ochelai   TERRA DELLA BORAD
                           P de S. Croce

Stadacona   Gamas

IL Disegno de discoperto
della nova Franza

Bolognini Zalterij
Anno MD LXVI

TERRA
IN COGNITA   AVACAL   LA NOVA   CANADA
                        FRANZA   PRO: LAGO
         APALCHEN   Stornatana
PAR   Taina TERRA DE BACCALOS
                                    LARCADIA   C.DeSpera
TE   Y de Orlan
         Sierra   Costa de modang   C.Ras
DI   Nevada QVIVIRA PRO: TERRA DE   R Fondo
                          Quiuira NORVMBEGA   MARE DEL LA
AS   R de Gathas
IA   C.de Molte Isole   NOVA FRANZA
         GOLFO
         CHINAN P.d.Fuego   CIVOLA HORA   C.S.Marco
Zangia   GRANATA   ISOLE AZORE
         C de Crus   LA FLORIDA
                                   La Bermuda
MARE DE MANGI   C.Rosso
                                              MARE DEL NORT   Meder
GIAPAN   C.S.Helena   ISOLE CANAR
                          S.Michel   LA   Bahama
                                      FLO
                                      RIDA
                          Apusalco   GOLFO   CVBA
                          Mistecat   MEXICANO
                    Tacantepech Crux Lamaica SPAGNOLA Virgine
MARE DEL SVR   Santo   C. de Iucatan   Anguita
                          Nicara   Las Barbuda
S. Bartolamio   Guardalupi
                                           S.Lucia   ISOLE DE CAPO
                          P de Cartagena   La Trinita
                    Panama
                          Darien
                    CA ST IGLIA DE   C.Bianco
                          LORO
Rio Benenenta

13   Part of Zaltieri's Map, 1566

Results of Early Explorations

Maps based on the discoveries made by Cartier and his predecessors were the best available for the next generation or more. The most important was that of the Dutchman, Gerardus Mercator, published in 1569. It introduced for the first time his famous method of map projection, while its American section portrayed accurately the extent of contemporary knowledge of that region. The Venetian map of Bolognino Zaltieri, on the other hand, shows what confusion still existed in many quarters regarding the St. Lawrence. It is a good example, too, of the wishful thinking of the age about a northern route to Asia and about the rumoured Strait of Anian.

From the standpoint of Canadian history, the main results of explorations to this date were: (1) quite full knowledge had been obtained of the Newfoundland-St. Lawrence coastal area with its great fishing banks but lack of rich kingdoms to conquer; (2) it had become almost certain that the Americas were separate from Asia, and that there was no seaway through them. This left only a quickening hope, especially in England, that there might be found a way around to the north better than that which Magellan had discovered to the south. It is noteworthy that the Zaltieri and similar maps were being published just at the time when Sir Humphrey Gilbert became interested in his great and disappointing search for the North-west Passage.

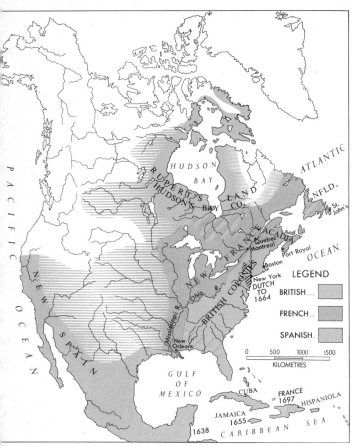

15 European Spheres of Interest

The seventeenth century was one of rapid development in North America in the course of which the Spaniards consolidated their control in the south and the English established flourishing settlements along the Atlantic coast, while the French colonized with greater difficulty and less success Acadia and the St. Lawrence Valley of Canada. Meanwhile, the four great entries into the interior of the continent were all discovered and opened. The St. Lawrence, the most immediately useful, permitted the French to establish a potentially great inland fur-trading empire, linked just as the century ended with the Mississippi entry as well. The Hudson River, explored by Henry Hudson in 1609, enabled his employers, the Dutch, to create an important agricultural and trading colony which they lost, however, to the English in 1664. Hudson Bay, also explored by Hudson (1610–11) but on behalf this time of his native England, became the centre of Hudson's Bay Company fur-trading after 1670. However, the Company's rights were vigorously disputed by the French who had reached the Bay by land. As the century ended, French-English rivalry over the fur trade of both Hudson Bay and the interior, and over the fisheries of Newfoundland, was becoming a dominant theme in North American history.

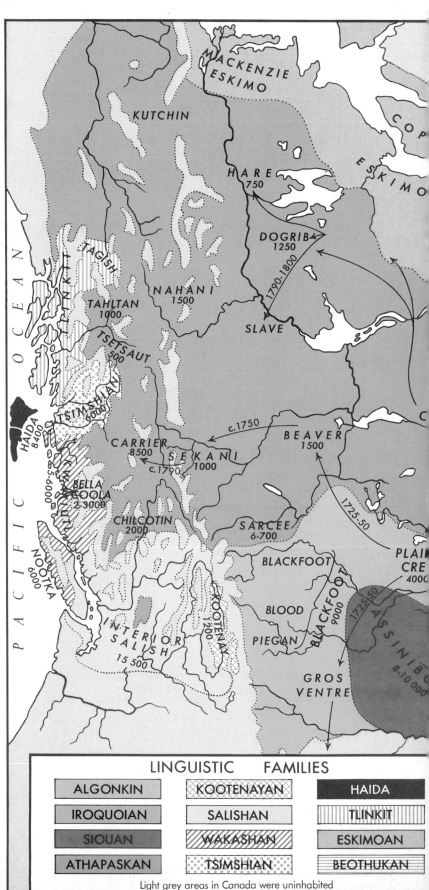

LINGUISTIC   FAMILIES

ALGONKIN	KOOTENAYAN	HAIDA
IROQUOIAN	SALISHAN	TLINKIT
SIOUAN	WAKASHAN	ESKIMOAN
ATHAPASKAN	TSIMSHIAN	BEOTHUKAN

Light grey areas in Canada were uninhabited

Most of the tribes met during the European penetration of the interior of North America were scattered and nomadic, and our knowledge about them is limited. The present map, therefore, attempts merely to show: (1) approximate locations of tribes at the time of their first contact with the Europeans, i.e. about the years 1525 east, and 1725 west, of 85° longitude; (2) estimated numbers in each tribe at that time; (3) the direction of certain major tribal migrations; (4) the linguistic grouping of tribes. This last is of importance as indicating probable earlier associations and movements of what may have become widely separated tribes. It is important too in making clear that the early explorers and fur traders faced no real language barrier in advancing from tribe to tribe all the way from the Atlantic to Hudson Bay and the foothills of the Rockies, since most of this vast region was occupied by Algonkian peoples.

ENTERING THE INTERIOR

GREENLAND ICE CAP

BYLOT AND BAFFIN 1616

DAVIS 1587

DAVIS 1585

FROBISHER 1576

FOXE 1631

MUNCK 1619-20

BUTTON 1612-13

JAMES 1631-32

HUDSON 1610-11

Cape Chidley

ATLANTI

OCEA

Belle I.

Cape Breton

100 0 100 200 300 400
KILOMETRES

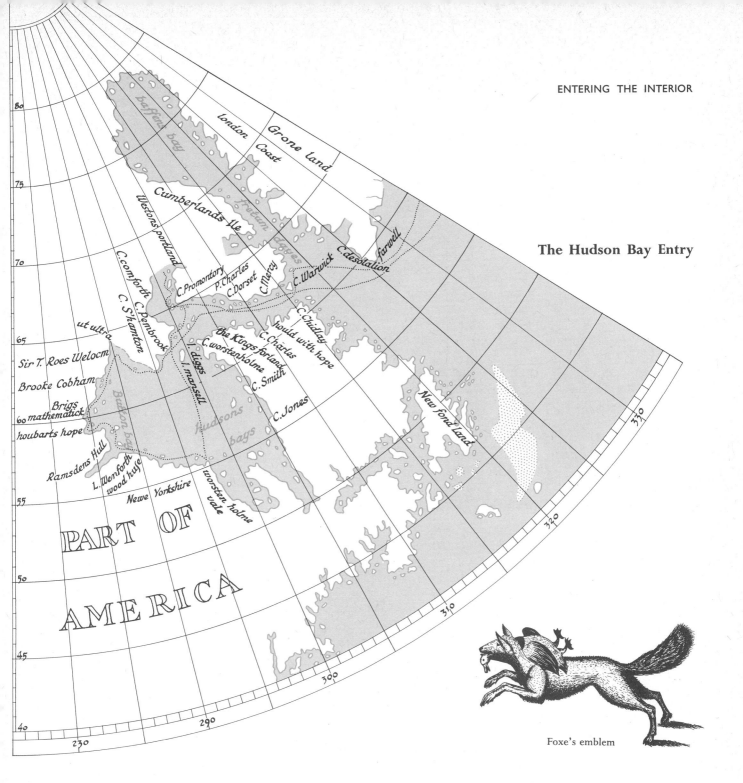

The Hudson Bay Entry

Foxe's emblem

17 The Search for a North-west Passage

Arctic explorers from Martin Frobisher to Foxe and James sought a North-west Passage to Asia, and instead gradually revealed one of the great entries to the North American continent. Except for the Dane, Jens Munck, all were English. The *Discovery,* the first of those famous Arctic ships that have become better known than many of their captains, made at least six of the voyages—under Waymouth in 1602, Hudson on his last great venture in 1610–11, Button in 1612–13, Gibbons in 1614, and Bylot and Baffin in 1615 and again in 1616.

Base map copyright Canadian Aero Service Limited, Ottawa

18 Part of Luke 'North West' Foxe's Map, 1635

The search for a North-west Passage ended for over a century with the rival voyages in 1631 of Luke 'North West' Foxe, a middle-aged seafarer of Hull, and Thomas James of Bristol. Both published books on their return, Foxe's containing his famous map, James' later inspiring Coleridge to write *The Ancient Mariner.*

The St. Lawrence Entry

19 Champlain's Explorations

Samuel de Champlain had visited the West Indies and served at the court of Henry IV of France before entering upon his remarkable career as explorer and colonizer in Acadia and Canada from 1603 until his death in 1635. His own travels included a trip up the St. Lawrence as far as the site of Hochelaga in 1603, investigation of the Bay of Fundy and its vicinity, 1604–7, ventures up the Richelieu into Lake Champlain in 1609 and up the Ottawa to Allumette Island in 1613, and finally a long round-about return journey (1615–16) through the Huron country and down south of Lake Ontario to make an attack on the Iroquois. His young *coureurs de bois* such as Etienne Brulé, Nicolas Vignau, and Jean Nicolet, and missionaries like Father Le Caron, supplied him with additional information. His professional skill as a geographer in piecing all his knowledge together in order to clarify much of the puzzling inter-relationship of the St. Lawrence, Richelieu, Ottawa, and Great Lakes waterways is displayed in his great map of 1632. The earlier map of 1612 shows how much he did not yet know at that time. A comparison of the almost contemporary Luke Foxe and Champlain maps reveals that the English and French were only vaguely familiar with each other's discoveries.

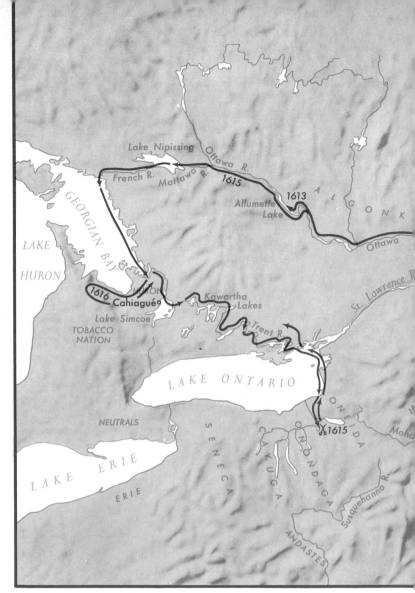

Base map copyright Canadian Aero Service Limited, Ottawa

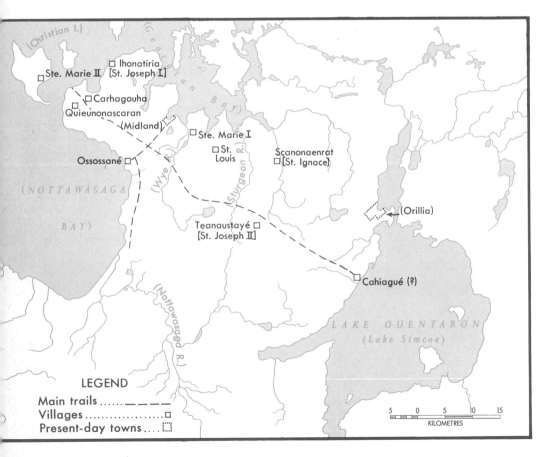

LEGEND

Main trails .... — — — —
Villages .... ☐
Present-day towns .... ☐

20 Huronia

The Hurons of Champlain's time, numbering perhaps 16 000, lived semi-agricultural lives in some eighteen villages huddled close together between Georgian Bay and Lake Simcoe. The villages were primitive and changed location from time to time for such reasons as the exhaustion of fuel supply and soil in the immediate vicinity. A Recollet, Father Le Caron, preceded Champlain into this region in the summer of 1615. The missionary work thus begun was continued after 1626 by the Jesuits who made a major effort to create a Christian Huronia comparable to the Christian societies they were currently establishing among South American Indians especially in Paraguay. In 1648 and 1649, however, the Huron nation was broken and dispersed by the Iroquois, among those tortured and slain being five Jesuits, including Jean de Brébeuf and Gabriel Lalemant.

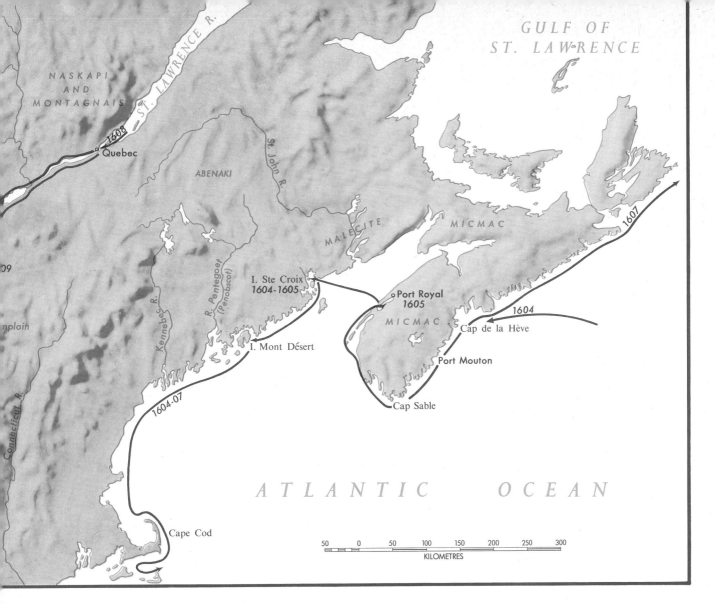

GULF OF
ST. LAWRENCE

NASKAPI
AND
MONTAGNAIS

1608
Quebec

ABENAKI

St. John R.

MALECITE

MICMAC

1607

I. Ste Croix
1604-1605

Port Royal
1605

MICMAC

1604

Cap de la Hève

R. Pentegoet (Penobscot)

Kennebec R.

I. Mont Désert

Port Mouton

1604-07

Cap Sable

Connecticut R.

ATLANTIC   OCEAN

Cape Cod

50   0   50   100   150   200   250   300
KILOMETRES

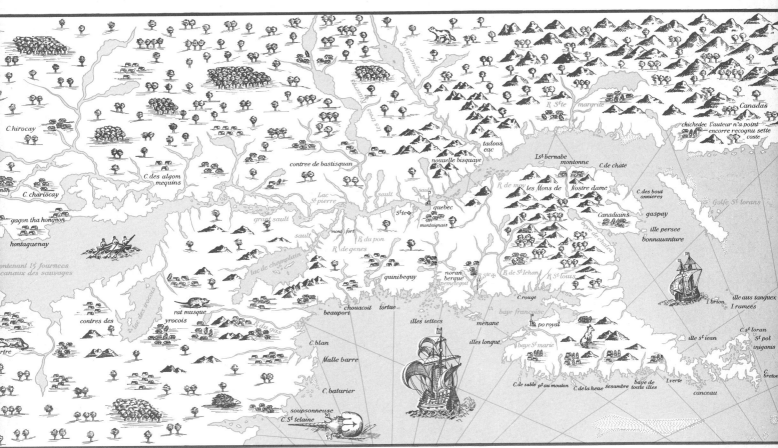

C. hirocay

C. chariocay

gagon tha hongnon

hontaguenay

contenant 15 journees
canaux des sauvages

contres des yrocois

C. des algom mequins

contree de bastisquan

Lac St pierre

grant sault

sault

mont fort

R. de genes

lac de champlain

rat musque yrocois

R. du gas

C. blan

Malle barre

C. baturier

soupsonneuse
C. St telaine

beauport

chouacoit   tortue

illes iettees

illes longue

quinibeguy

noran berque penelegoy

St te

montaignas

quebec

sault

R. du pon

tadous eac

nouuelle bisquaye

R. Ste   margrite

R. de may

les Mons de Nostre dame

Lst bernabe montonne

C. de chate

Canaduains

C. rouge

ménane

po royal

baye francoise

baye St marie

C. de sable p.t au mouton

C. de la heue   sesambre

Canadas

chichedec l'auteur n'a point
encorre recognu sette
coste

C. des bout
onnieres

Golfe St lorans

gaspay

ille persee

bonnauanture

I. brion

ille aus tanguex
I ramees

ille St iean

C. St loran
St pol
iniganis

baye de
toute illes

Lverte

canceau

C. breton

21   Part of Champlain's 1612 Map   ENTERING THE INTERIOR

MER DV NORT GLACIALLE

C. Worsnam

C. Harles

N O V V E L L E   F R A N C E

Sault

Lac des   Biserenis

La Nation des Puans

Petite nation des Algommeguins

Isle où il y a une mine de cuivre

Sault

Sault

Sault

Algomme guins

Les trois rivieres

Sault

Sault

Mer douce

Grande Lac

Sault

Descouvertures de ce grand lac, et de toutes ses terres depuis le sault S. Louis par le st de Champlain, es années 1614, et 1615, iusques en t'an 1618.

Lieu ou il y a forse & Cerfs

Sault

Sault

Hurons

Lac de Champlain

Lac St Louis

Cheueux releuez Gens de Petun

Chouai Port aus

Grande riviere qui vient du mi dy

Hiro cois

Sain- tonge

Cap des Isles
Beau port
Port St Louis

Les gens de feu assistagueron ons

La nation neutre

Hiro cois

Cap blan
Malle barre

R aux escailles

Port fortune

Antouoronons

Habitation des sauvages maniganaticou it

Riviere de Champlain

Nation ou il y a quantité de beuffles

Carantouann ais

Baye de nostre Dame

Riviere des trettes

Isle de l'Ascension

Virginia

Carte de la nouvelle france, avgmentée depuis la derniere, servant a la navigation faicte en son vray Meridien, par le st de Champlain Capitaine pour le Roy en la Marine; lequel depuis l'an 1603 iusques en l'année 1629, a descouvert plusieurs costes, terres, lacs, rivieres, et Nations de sauvages, par cy devant incognutes, comme il se voit en ses relations quil a faict Imprimer en 1632 ou il se voit cette marque ce sont habitations qu'ont faict les françois.

C. Charles
C. Henry

| 83 | 284 | 285 | 286 | 287 | 288 | 289 | 290 | 291 | 292 | 293 | 294 | 295 | 296 | 297 | 298 | 299 | 300 | 301 | 302 | 303 | 304 | 305 | 306 | 307 | 308 |

22   Champlain's 1632 Map

annes fort landt
C. Elizabeth
Lomle Inlet
Groenlan dia

Terres de la Brador

Esquimaux Brest Croix blanche
Belle isle
Isle fichot
Cap de grat
Cap rouge
Groye
La grande baye

Baye dorge
Les isles aux Chauaux Isle aux apouois
Baye blanche
C. St Iean
Sauvages Bersiam iste
Baye de rochers
Basse de Ste Marie Port aux Ours Le Golphe St Laurens
Port neuf
Baye des ballaines
Saincte Margueritte C. des rosiers Anticosty Terre neuve
Isles des fougues
Isle de moy
C. de bonne viste
C. dechate Montana C. dechate Monts nostre Dame Gaspay
Les quemain Baye des molues
Tadousac St Barnabé Isle persee Isle de bacallos
Le Bic Isle bonaventure Baye Ste Claire
Baye de Chaleu Ban des orphelins Isle aux oyseaux Baye de la Conception
Miscou Cap de ray Cap Ste Fresaye
Tregatay Isle ramee Ste Claire Frinouse
Nouvelle France La baye du petit J. St Paul Rocher Isles despoirs
mitamichy La Magdelene C. St Laurens Cap de raze
La R. Ste Iean Isle St Iean Niganis
C. des mines Cap Enfumé Isles St Pierre Rochers
Ste Croix Gransibou Le grand banc
Baye francoise Cap breton Bane vert
Menane C. de Poitrincourt Port aux Anglois
Port royal Souricois Cap St Antoine Banquereaux
Baye Ste Marie Ste Margueritte Canceau
Isle verte Port de savalette
Sesambre Baye de toute isles
Port de Ste Helaine
Isle des martures
Cap fourchu C. de la heve
Port au mouton
C. negre
Cap de Sable Isle de Sable
Isles aux loups marins

5 10 20 30 40 50 60 70 80 90 100

Faicte l'an 1632 parte sieur de Champlain

312 313 314 315 316 317 318 319 320 321 322 323 324 325 326 327 328 229 230 231 232 233 234 235 236 23

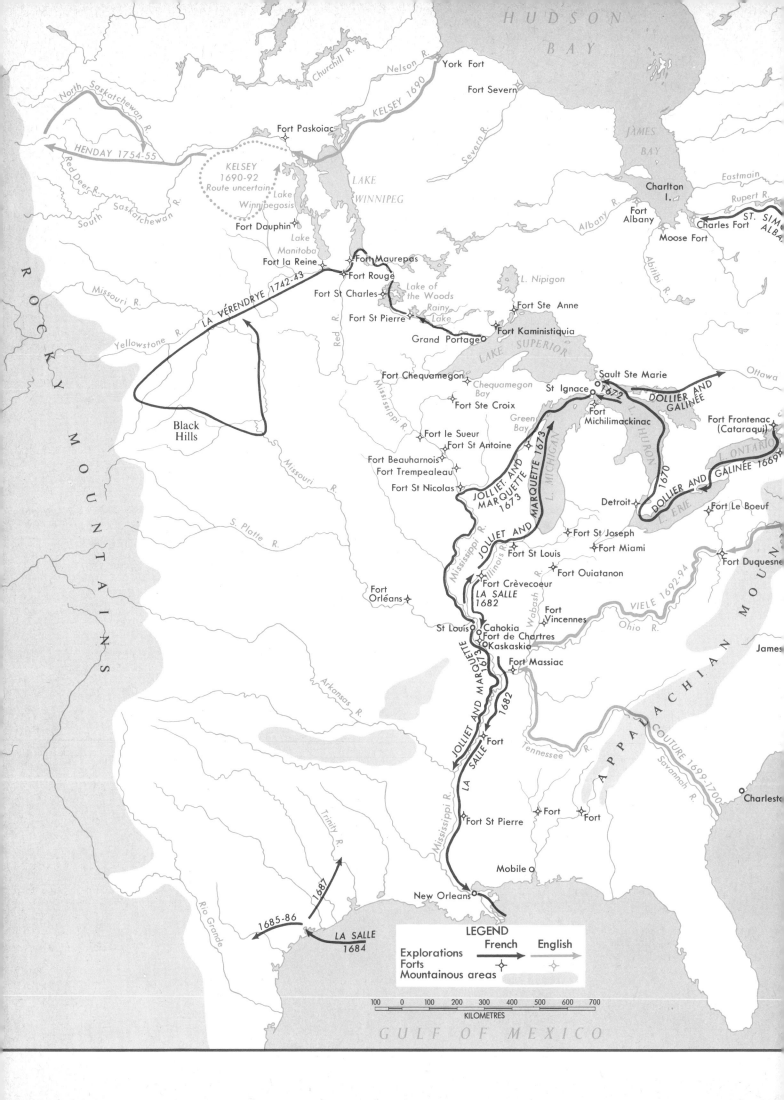

HUDSON BAY

JAMES BAY

York Fort

Fort Severn

KELSEY 1690

Churchill R.

Nelson R.

North Saskatchewan R.

HENDAY 1754-55

Red Deer R.

Fort Paskoiac

KELSEY 1690-92
Route uncertain

Lake Winnipegosis

South Saskatchewan

Missouri R.

Fort Dauphin

Lake Manitoba

LAKE WINNIPEG

Charlton I.

Eastmain R.

Rupert R.

ST. SIM

Fort Albany

Charles Fort

ALBA

Moose Fort

Fort la Reine

Fort Maurepas

Fort Rouge

LA VÉRENDRYE 1742-43

Fort St Charles

Lake of the Woods

Fort St Pierre

Rainy Lake

Red R.

L. Nipigon

Fort Ste Anne

Albany R.

Abitibi R.

Yellowstone R.

Black Hills

Grand Portage

Fort Kaministiquia

LAKE SUPERIOR

ROCKY MOUNTAINS

Missouri R.

Fort Chequamegon

Chequamegon Bay

Fort Ste Croix

Fort le Sueur

Fort St Antoine

Fort Beauharnois

Fort Trempealeau

Fort St Nicolas

JOLLIET AND MARQUETTE 1673

Mississippi R.

Green Bay

Sault Ste Marie

St Ignace   1672

DOLLIER AND GALINÉE

Fort Michilimackinac

L. HURON

1670

Ottawa R.

Fort Frontenac (Cataraqui)

L. ONTARIO

DOLLIER AND GALINÉE 1669

JOLLIET AND MARQUETTE 1673

L. MICHIGAN

Detroit

DOLLIER AND GALINÉE

L. ERIE

Fort Le Boeuf

JOLLIET AND MARQUETTE 1673

Fort St Joseph

Fort Miami

Fort St Louis

Fort Ouiatanon

Fort Crèvecoeur
LA SALLE 1682

VIELE 1692-94

Fort Duquesne

S. Platte R.

Fort Orléans

Illinois R.

Fort Vincennes

Wabash R.

Ohio R.

St Louis

Cahokia

Fort de Chartres

Kaskaskia

Fort Massiac

Arkansas R.

JOLLIET AND MARQUETTE 1673

LA SALLE 1682

Tennessee R.

APPALACHIAN MOUN

COUTURE 1699-1700

James

Savannah R.

Charlesto

Mississippi R.

LA SALLE 1682

Fort St Pierre

Fort

Fort

Rio Grande

Trinity R.

1687

1685-86

New Orleans

Mobile o

LA SALLE 1684

LEGEND

Explorations   French   English
Forts
Mountainous areas

100   0   100   200   300   400   500   600   700
KILOMETRES

GULF OF MEXICO

20

PART TWO EXPLORATION AND DEVELOPMENT TO 1763

SECTION 3 GROWTH AND CONFLICT

23 Exploration and Fur Trade in the Interior

Champlain, having founded Quebec in 1608 and nursed it through its infancy, was obliged to surrender it in 1629 to an English force under David Kirke and was not able to return until after the restoration of peace in 1632. Meanwhile, in Acadia, the long conflict between English and French had begun even earlier with Samuel Argall's raids on French settlements in 1613 and James I's grant of 'Nova Scotia' to Sir William Alexander in 1621. In 1759, one hundred and thirty years after Kirke, Wolfe captured Quebec again, bringing the struggle to its culmination. Finally with peace in 1763 Canada and adjacent possessions were transferred to British rule.

The long-standing hostility of France and Britain in Europe and other parts of the world was heightened in North America by rivalry over the Newfoundland fisheries and the fur trade of the continental interior. With regard to the latter the French, following the example of Champlain and encouraged by missionary zeal and inviting waterways branching inward from Montreal, took an early lead. During the seventeenth century they not only explored the whole Great Lake region but reached out as well to Hudson Bay and the mouth of the Mississippi. The curbing of the Iroquois in 1666 by the Marquis de Tracy cleared the way for especially rapid progress after that date, stimulated by Colbert, Talon, and Frontenac. In the eighteenth century, the La Vérendryes and others led the way out into the Great Plains.

The English were comparatively slow in pushing inland from Hudson Bay or the Atlantic seaboard, and what they did accomplish was sometimes with the assistance of renegade Frenchmen like Radisson and Jean Couture and Dutchmen like Viele. Geographic and other factors, however, made their fur traders, whether operating from Hudson Bay or the Hudson River, dangerous competitors of the more energetic French. Only a few representative and reasonably well-recorded journeys can be shown with advantage on a map, but this must not be allowed to obscure the importance of Radisson, Groseilliers, Dulhut, Tonti, and countless others—missionaries, *coureurs de bois*, and Indian guides, many completely unknown to history—who played their part in the discovery of the continent.

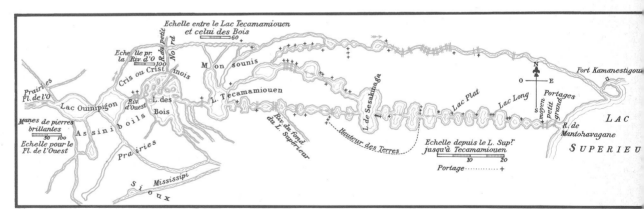

24 The Ochagach Map

Some of the problems of the explorers can be understood when the map of La Vérendrye's Indian guide Ochagach is compared with the modern representation of the waterways between Lake Superior and Lake Winnipeg included in Map 23 and in greater detail in Map 62. Ochagach was probably superior to most Indian guides, but he was quite vague about distance and direction and hopeful in his assurances that La Vérendrye would find the westward-flowing rivers he sought and also mountains of shining stones.

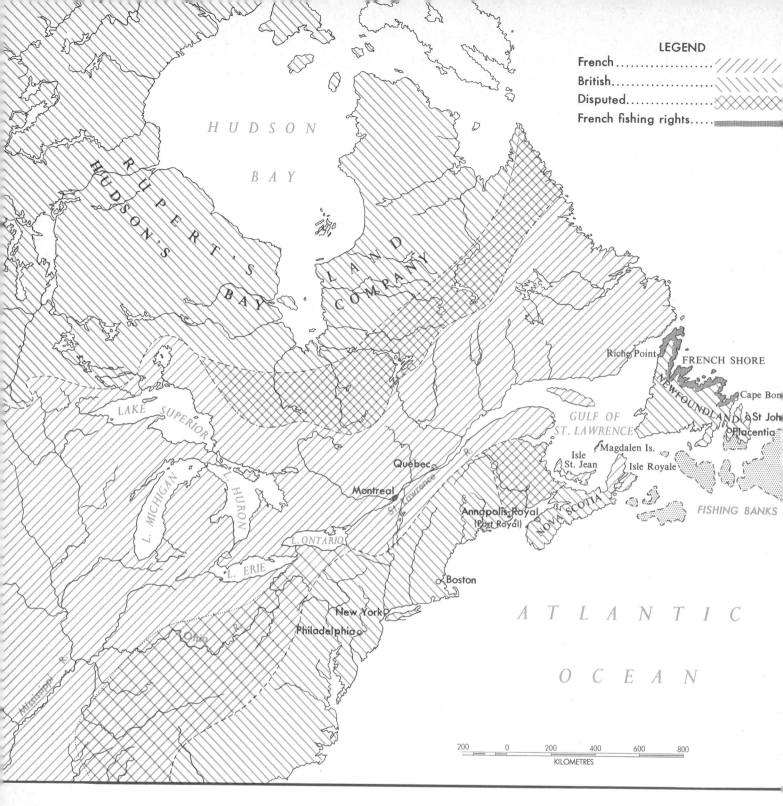

25 The Treaty of Utrecht, 1713

France's first permanent territorial losses in North America were acknowledged in the Treaty of Utrecht which ended the War of the Spanish Succession (Queen Anne's War) in 1713. By it France recognized British ownership of the Hudson Bay region, Newfoundland, and 'all Nova Scotia or Acadie, with its ancient boundaries, as also the city of Port Royal'. Specifically retained by France were the islands of the Gulf of St. Lawrence including Isle Royale (Cape Breton) and also certain fishing rights along the northward shores of Newfoundland be-

tween Cape Bonavista and Riche Point. The special interests of both countries in respect to the territories of their Indian allies were admitted, the Iroquois territories being definitely assigned to the British sphere. A provision that commissioners be appointed to determine the various boundaries more exactly proved ineffective, and when the next war began the limits of the Hudson's Bay Territories remained in dispute and French occupation of what is now New Brunswick still continued.

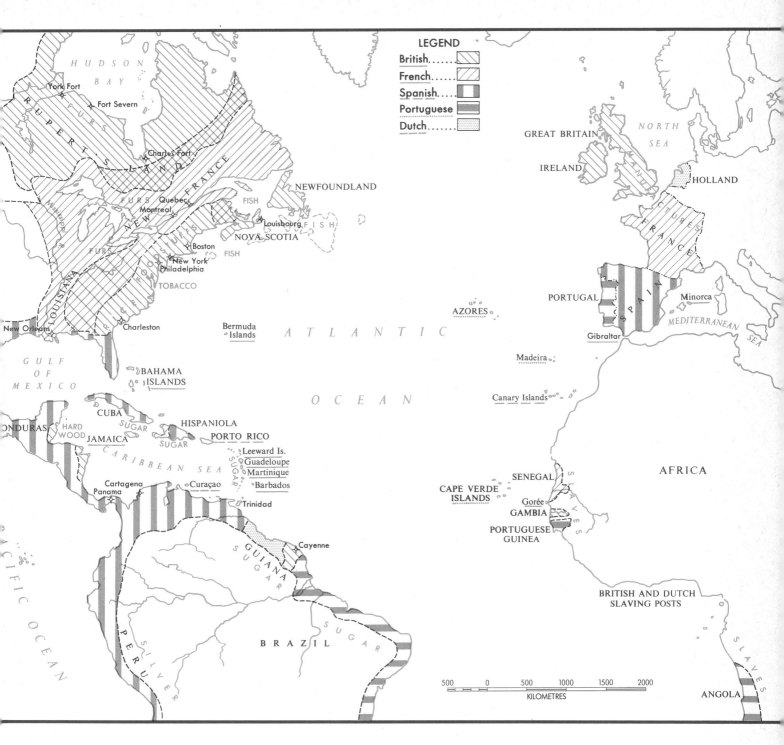

26 Atlantic Trading Rivalries

Eighteenth-century wars between Britain and
France were by no means confined to border
clashes in North America. They were world-
wide struggles for commercial and colonial
supremacy, fought in eastern oceans and
India as well as in Europe and the Atlantic
region. In the latter the furs and fish of
Canada were among the principal prizes at
stake, along with the sugar of the West
Indies and the slave trade of Africa.

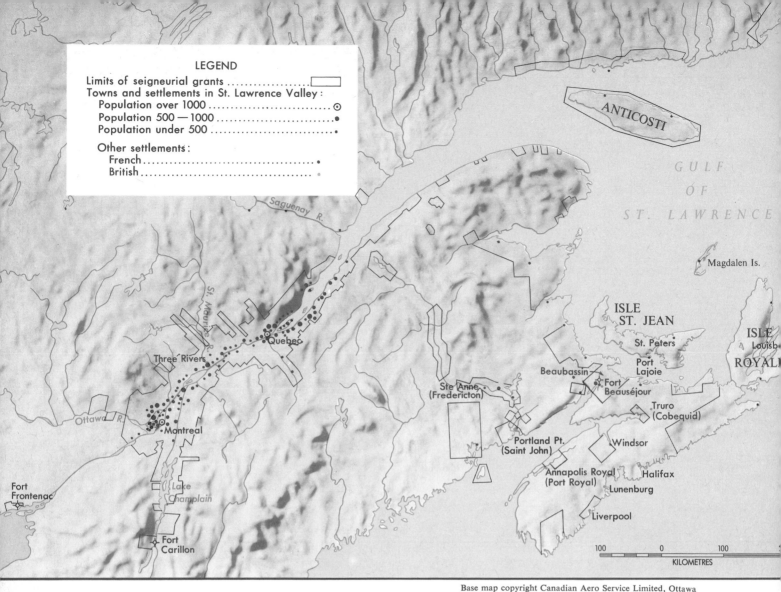

28   The Growth of Population

NOTE:
Figures in italics are estimates; other figures are based on censuses or other reasonably reliable sources.

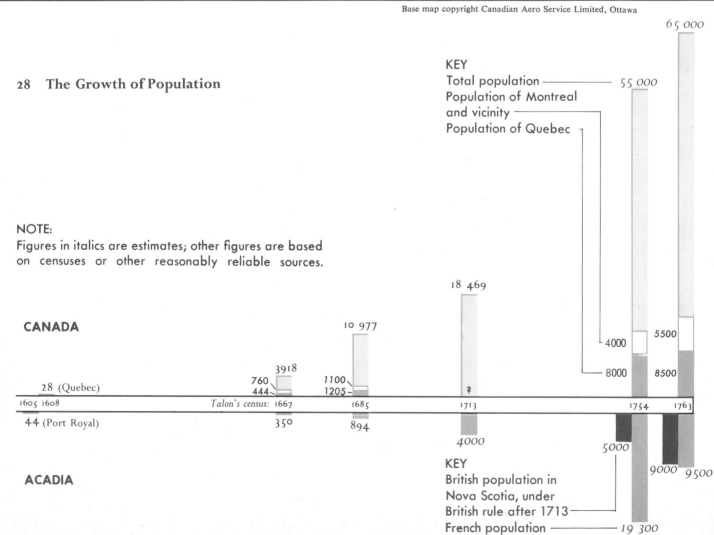

KEY
Total population ——————— *55 000*
Population of Montreal
and vicinity ———————
Population of Quebec

65 000

CANADA

18 469

10 977

3918
760
444

28 (Quebec)

4000
5500
8000
8500

1605 1608   *Talon's census:* 1667   1685   1713   1754   1763

1100
1205

44 (Port Royal)   *350*   894

4000

5000

ACADIA

9000 *9500*

KEY
British population in
Nova Scotia, under
British rule after 1713 ———
French population ——————— *19 300*

A major disadvantage of the French in North America was the extent to which they were outnumbered by the British to the south. The spectacular achievements of their fur traders and explorers were not matched by their 'habitant' farmers who were adding only slowly to the area under cultivation in the St. Lawrence lowlands of Canada and in a few parts of Acadia, notably on the tidal marshlands at the head of the Bay of Fundy, on Isle St. Jean (Prince Edward Island), and around Port Royal.

The land-holding system was seigneurial, based on that of France. Grants of some sixty seigneuries had been made before 1663; more than that number followed rapidly during the next nine years when Jean Talon was intendant, and others were added during the remainder of the French régime and even in a few cases after the British conquest. The last grant was in 1788, and the system was abolished in 1854. Seigneurs were supposed to see to the clearing and settlement of their land, but few were able to satisfy fully these requirements, especially in the early days.

Settlement clung to the coasts and river banks for ease of transportation. The market for farm products, however, was never great —the supply of a few towns and some fishermen and fur traders—although in later years of mounting wars with the British it expanded in line with the needs of reinforced garrisons at Quebec, Louisbourg, Beauséjour, and other forts. Shipbuilding and the productive but unprofitable iron forges on the St. Maurice near Three Rivers were the only significant secondary industries, apart from home spinning and weaving and local milling. The fur trade itself, however colourful, was always an uncertain source of wealth and employment. All of this contrasted alarmingly with the rapid and solid progress of the British colonies.

Population records for the French régime are amazingly detailed and show that growth was very slow before 1663. A period of more rapid expansion followed, due mainly to the efforts of Jean Talon, intendant from 1663 to 1672, and to the support he received from his masters, Louis XIV and Colbert. In the eighteenth century progress continued at a steady but by no means spectacular pace. The total French population (Canadian and Acadian) was still less than 80 000 in 1763 and seemed very small indeed when compared with the 1 500 000 in the British colonies to the south. The largest towns, Quebec and Montreal, were similarly dwarfed by Boston, New York, and Philadelphia.

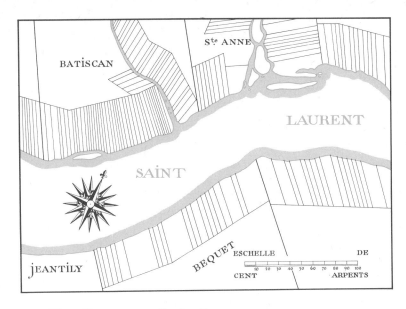

29 The Customary Strip Farms

The farms into which the seigneuries were divided customarily took the form of narrow strips of land so that each could have its own river frontage and its own woodlot in back. The habitants lived, as a result, in *côtes* or scattered lines of houses along the river banks. To suggest the advantage of more compact communities in the traditional French pattern, Talon founded three 'round' villages near Quebec, but his example was not followed.

30 Talon's Round Villages

GROWTH
AND CONFLICT

Royal Canadian Air Force photograph

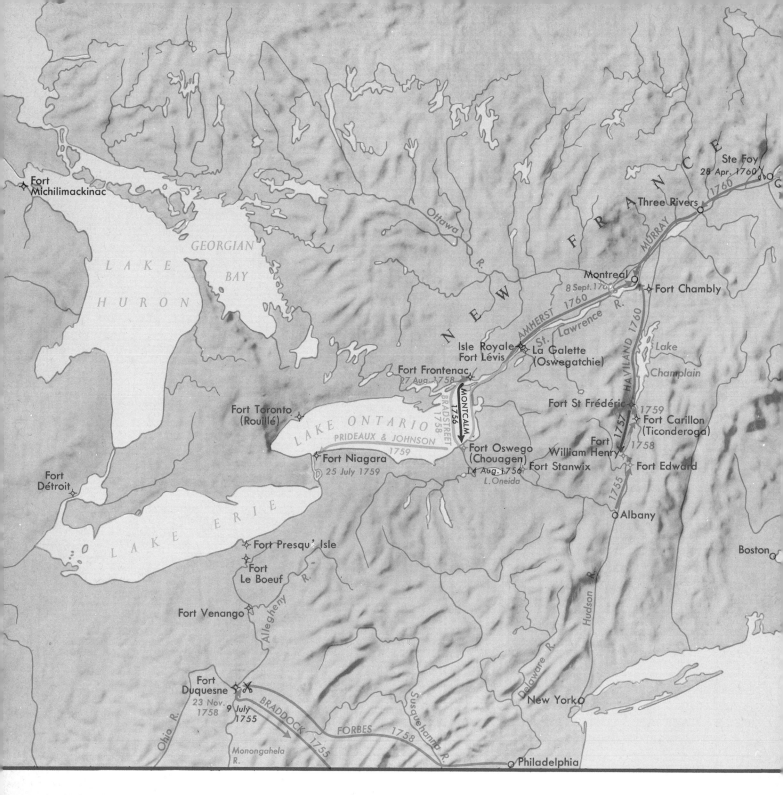

31   The Seven Years' War

The finally decisive struggle between the French and British in North America was the Seven Years' War. In 1754, two years before the formal declaration of war in Europe, conflict began in North America when the French from Canada and the English from Virginia clashed in rival attempts to occupy the rich Ohio Valley. The French built Fort Duquesne at the strategic forks of the Ohio, where the Allegheny and the Monongahela come together, and forced the surrender of a small English expedition under George Washington at nearby Fort Necessity (July 3). For the next five years, except when winter pre-

vented all but minor skirmishes, fighting continued usually on all three fronts: (1) in the west, in the Ohio country and around Lake Erie and Lake Ontario; (2) in the centre, where the Hudson-Champlain-Richelieu waterway constituted the great 'warpath of nations'; and (3) in the north-eastward approaches to Canada, the St. Lawrence gulf and river region.

The main events were as follows:
1755. In the west, the British commander-in-chief, Braddock, was ambushed and defeated approaching Fort Duquesne (July 9); in the centre, the British were victorious in fighting beside Lake George (September 8)

but failed in their object of capturing Fort St. Frédéric (Crown Point); in the east, they captured Fort Beauséjour (June 16) and expelled the Acadians. That autumn the French began building Fort Carillon (Ticonderoga) and the English Fort William Henry and Fort Edward.
1756. England formally declared war on France (May 17). Montcalm, the new French commander-in-chief, captured and destroyed Fort Oswego (Chouagen) on August 14.
1757. Montcalm captured Fort William Henry (August 9); many of the inhabitants were killed in subsequent Indian attacks.

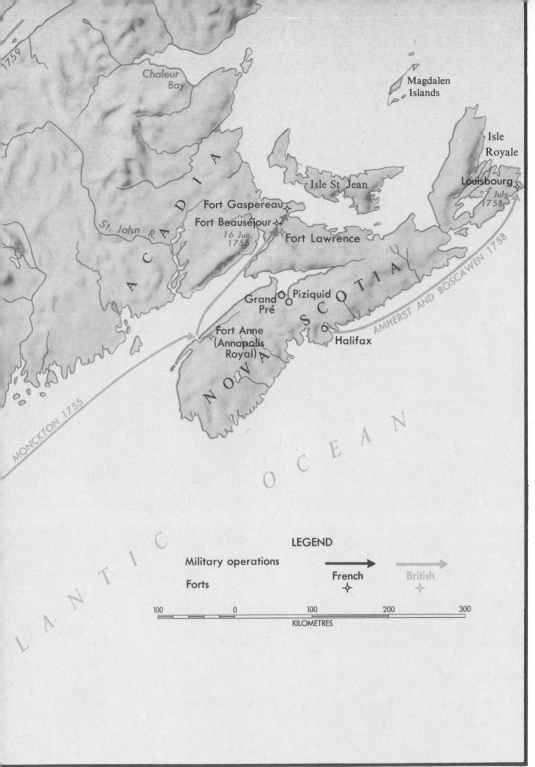

Base map copyright Canadian Aero Service Limited, Ottawa

LEGEND

Military operations

Forts

French ✦

British ✦

1758. Abercromby was repulsed in a major attack on Fort Carillon (July 8), but Amherst, Wolfe, and Admiral Boscawen captured Louisbourg (July 27), Bradstreet raided and destroyed Fort Frontenac (August 25), and Forbes forced the French evacuation of Fort Duquesne (November 23).

1759. The British captured Fort Niagara (July 25) and obliged the French to withdraw without fighting from Fort Carillon (July 26) and Fort St. Frédéric (August 4). But for Amherst's caution, the British advance might have continued as far as Montreal in the weeks that followed. Meanwhile, in the St. Lawrence region,

Admiral Saunders' fleet had succeeded in transporting Wolfe's army to Quebec (June 27) where, after a long summer's siege, it won the Battle of the Plains of Abraham (September 13) and entered the city (September 18).

1760. A brave attempt by Lévis to recapture Quebec led to a British defeat in the Battle of Ste. Foy (April 28), after which Murray retired behind the city walls and withstood siege until the British fleet arrived (May 9–16). Murray, Amherst, and Haviland then converged on Montreal where the final capitulation of New France took place (September 8).

32   The Warpath of Nations

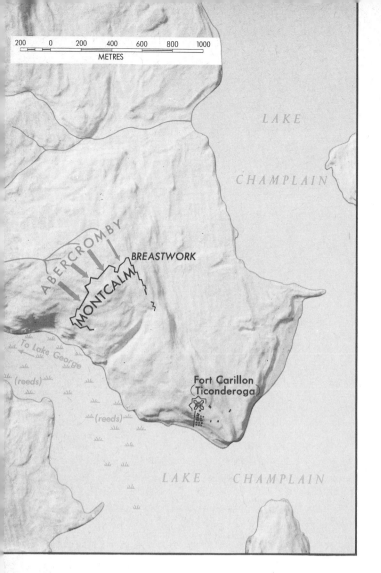

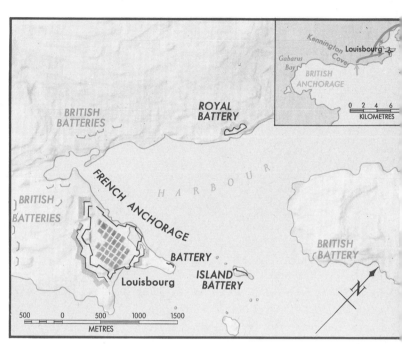

33 Defence of Fort Carillon, 1758

Because of the disrepair of Fort Carillon, Montcalm hastily erected advance defences of earthworks surmounted by felled trees, and from these repulsed with smaller numbers a frontal assault prematurely launched by the incompetent Abercromby.

An abattis

34 Siege of Louisbourg, 1758

After a feebly resisted landing in Gabarus Bay (June 8) and in spite of difficult swampy approaches and French sorties, the British succeeded, with much effort, in placing themselves in position to bombard Louisbourg from several points on land as well as from the ships of their fleet. Pounded for eight days by heavy fire and reduced to ruin, the fort surrendered to Amherst (July 27).

35 Siege of Quebec, 1759

With Saunders' fleet safely anchored in the shelter of the Island of Orleans (June 27), Wolfe proceeded to establish three camps—a base camp on the island itself, a bombardment site at Point Lévis opposite Quebec, and his own headquarters north-east of the Montmorency River. After much vacillation he launched a major attack (July 31) in an attempt to force a way through to Quebec along the Beauport shore. Repulsed by the French holding the precipitous Montmorency Heights, he decided finally, with the approach of autumn, to take his brigadiers' advice to slip past Quebec and at least cut the French line of food supply from the west. In fact, surprise, on which the plan depended, was complete, and after the landing at Anse au Foulon and a brisk battle on the Plains of Abraham (September 13) in which he and Montcalm were both fatally wounded, the city was taken (September 18).

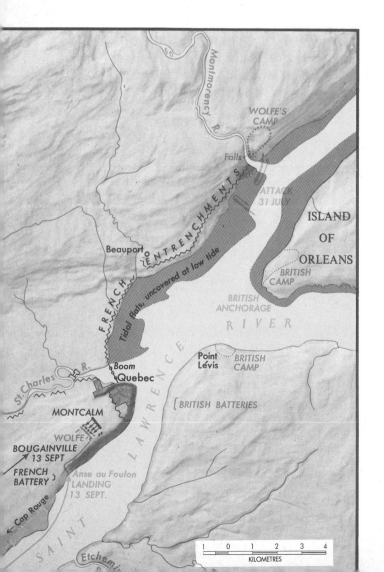

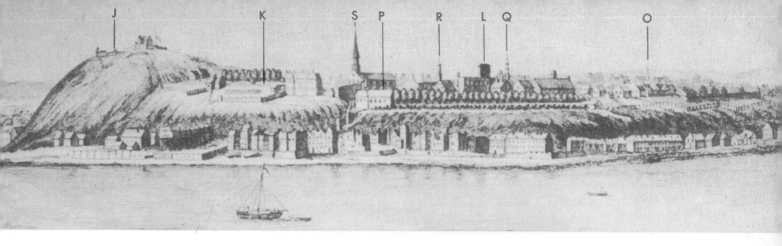

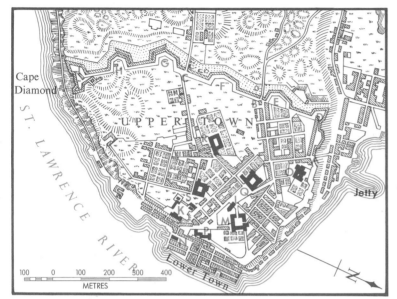

36–37　Quebec, 1763

A Palace Gate
B St. John's Gate
C St. Louis Gate
D Potasse Bastion
E St. John's Bastion
F Ste. Ursule Bastion
G St. Louis Bastion
H La Glacière Bastion
J Cape Diamond Bastion
K Fort St. Louis
L The Cathedral (in ruins)
M The Seminary
N Church of the Lower Town (Notre Dame des Victoires)
O Hôtel Dieu
P The Bishop's Palace
Q The Jesuits
R The Ursulines
S The Recollets

GROWTH AND CONFLICT

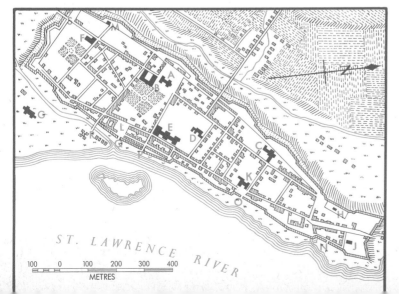

38–39　Montreal, 1763

A Parish Church
B Sulpician Seminary
C The Jesuits
D Sisters of the Congregation
E Their hospital
F The Recollets
G Hôtel Dieu
H The Fort
J Arsenal
K Governor's House and Parade
L The Market
M Powder Magazine
N Sally port
O Water Gate
P St. Mary's Gate
Q Market Gate
R The Small Gate
S Recollets' Gate

LEGEND

British ....

Spanish ....

French ....

French fishing rights ....

Russian ....

40 The Treaty of Paris, 1763

The Treaty of Paris, signed by Great Britain, France, Spain, and Portugal on February 10, 1763, ended the West European and colonial phases of the Seven Years War, and marked the withdrawal of France from the mainland of North America. In the north-eastern part of the continent, France ceded to Britain all territories that had remained to her after the Treaty of Utrecht, i.e. Canada and what is now New Brunswick, together with adjacent islands, including Isle Royale (Cape Breton) and Isle St. Jean (Prince Edward Island). She retained the fishing rights in Newfoundland guaranteed by the Treaty of Utrecht, and received as well the islands of St. Pierre and Miquelon for use as unfortified fishing bases. In the centre and south, France and Spain gave up all their territories east of the Mississippi from the Great Lakes to Florida, except New Orleans. The latter and French lands west of the Mississippi (Louisiana) had already been transferred to Spain by the secret Treaty of San Ildefonso (November 3, 1762). Various West Indian islands were restored to their previous owners. The general effect of the treaty was that for a time after 1763, Britain was in possession of the whole eastern half of the continent, France was virtually eliminated as a North American power, and the somewhat enlarged Spanish territories became concentrated in the south-west. The north-west remained as yet almost unknown, except for recent Russian advances down the Alaskan coast.

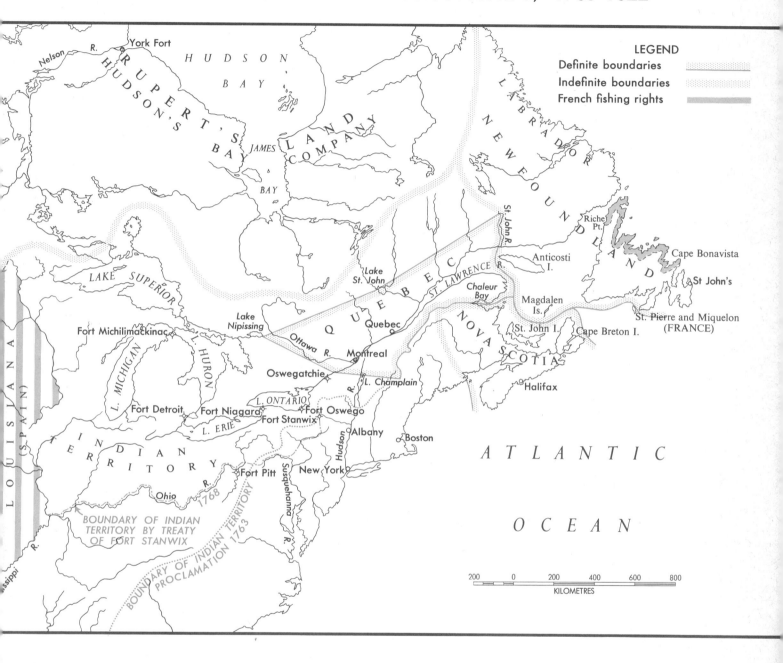

41   The Royal Proclamation of 1763

On October 7, 1763, the Government of George III issued a Proclamation establishing the boundaries and governments of territories acquired in the Treaty of Paris. It (1) created a new colony, Quebec, whose boundary followed Quebec's St. John River, passed from its headwaters through Lake St. John to Lake Nipissing and to the St. Lawrence at the 45th parallel just above Montreal, then turned back eastward along that parallel, the height of land, and along the north shore of Chaleur Bay, as does the present boundary of the Province of Quebec, and crossed west of Anticosti to the mouth of the St. John River; (2) assumed that Nova Scotia included what is now New Brunswick (as Britain had claimed unsuccessfully since 1713) and added to it Cape Breton and St. Jean or St. John (later Prince Edward) Islands; (3) annexed to Newfoundland the coast of Labrador from the St. John River to Hudson Strait and also Anticosti and the Magdalen Islands in order to assure unified control of the gulf and coastal fisheries, these being considered 'the most obvious advantages arising from the Cessions'; (4) set aside all lands west and north of rivers flowing into the Atlantic, except those already granted to the Hudson's Bay Company or included in Quebec, to be Indian Territories from which settlement would be excluded and in which trade could be carried on only under licence. In the next few years, several Indian treaties, notably that with the Iroquois at Fort Stanwix (1768) took the limits of settlement slightly westward.

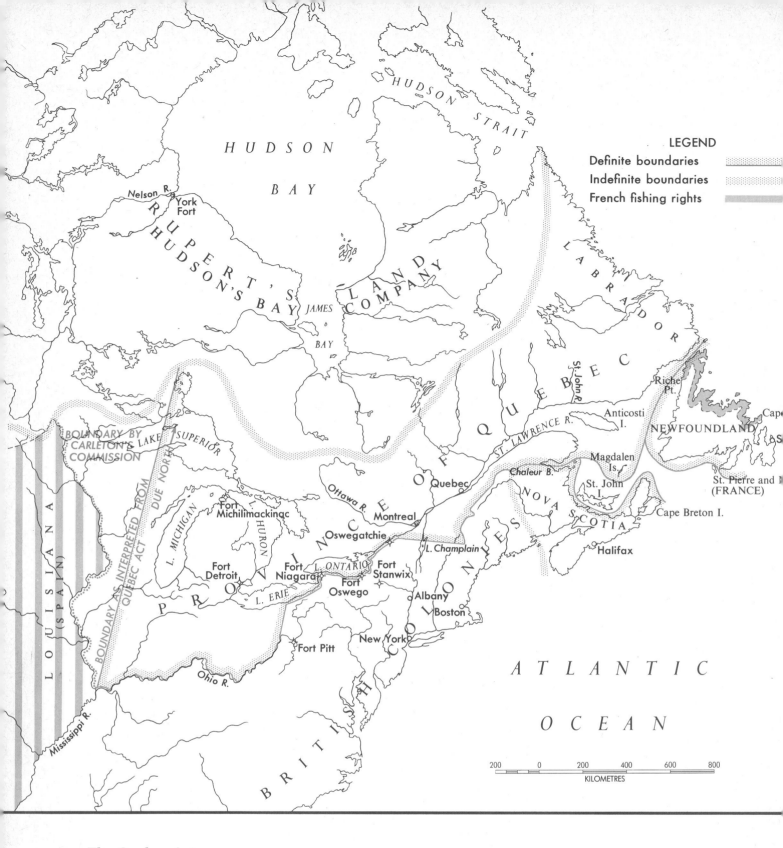

LEGEND
Definite boundaries
Indefinite boundaries
French fishing rights

HUDSON STRAIT

HUDSON

BAY

RUPERT'S

HUDSON'S BAY

Nelson R.

York
Fort

JAMES

BAY

LAND COMPANY

LABRADOR

St. John R.

Riche
Pt.

Anticosti
I.

NEWFOUNDLAND

Cape
Ras

BOUNDARY BY
CARLETON'S
COMMISSION

LAKE SUPERIOR

DUE NORTH

BOUNDARY AS INTERPRETED FROM
QUEBEC ACT

PROVINCE

OF

QUEBEC

ST. LAWRENCE R.

Magdalen
Is.

St. Pierre and
(FRANCE)

Chaleur B.

St. John
I.

L. MICHIGAN

L. HURON

Fort
Michilimackinac

Ottawa R.

Quebec

Montreal

NOVA SCOTIA

Cape Breton I.

LOUISIANA
(SPAIN)

Oswegatchie

L. Champlain

Halifax

Fort
Detroit

L. ONTARIO

Fort
Niagara

L. ERIE

Fort
Stanwix

Fort
Oswego

Albany

Boston

Fort Pitt

New York

BRITISH COLONIES

Ohio R.

Mississippi R.

ATLANTIC

OCEAN

200   0   200   400   600   800
KILOMETRES

42   The Quebec Act, 1774

The Quebec Act, May 20, 1774, brought both the fisheries of the Gulf of St. Lawrence and the fur trade of the interior within the jurisdiction of the Quebec Government by annexing to that province (1) Labrador, Anticosti, and the Magdalen Islands, previously belonging to Newfoundland, and (2) the Indian Territories south-westward to the junction of the Ohio and Mississippi and thence 'Northward to the Southern Boundary' of the Hudson's Bay Company's lands.

This second provision, although followed by specific provisions to safeguard existing boundaries and rights of the older British colonies, added nevertheless to their growing discontent by limiting their further westward expansion. Moreover, Guy Carleton's commission as governor of Quebec some months later defined the boundary from the Ohio as running northward along the Mississippi, and thus placed it farther west than if it had run due northward. A century later this

apparent discrepancy, clearly unintentiona and due to careless wording of the final draf of the Act, led to a vigorous boundary dis pute between Manitoba and Ontario, finall decided in favour of the latter by the Judicia Committee of the Privy Council in 1884 (se Maps 97 and 98). Meanwhile St. Joh Island (Prince Edward Island after 1799 was given separate government in 1769 at th request of the proprietors among whom i had been divided in 1767 (see Map 78).

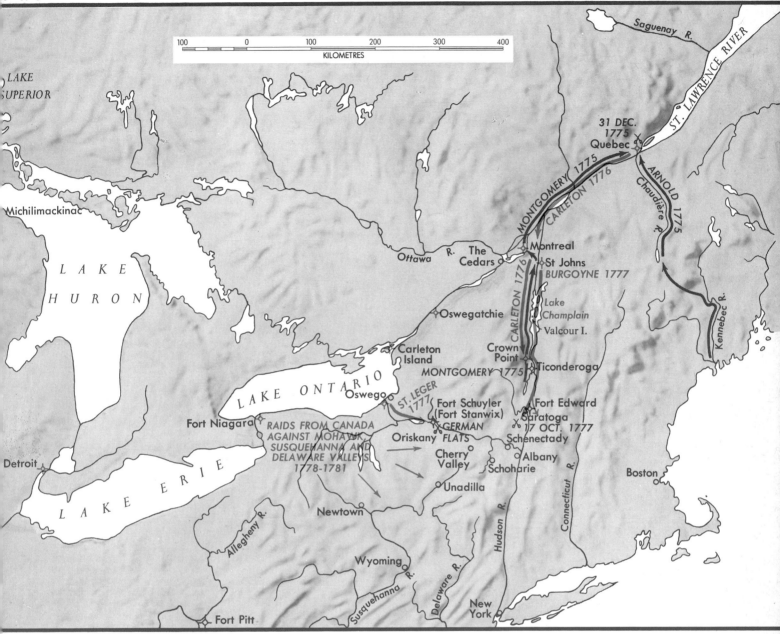

43 The American Revolutionary War, 1775–83

The first shots of the American Revolutionary War at Lexington and Concord (April 19, 1775) near Boston were followed by an attempt to win over the traditional enemy, Canada, first by an appeal from the Second Continental Congress and then by invasion. The invasion, a two-pronged attack led by Richard Montgomery and Benedict Arnold, was the main event of the first year of war apart from the Battle of Bunker Hill. After the heroic defence and final surrender of St. Johns (September 4–November 3), it culminated in an unsuccessful assault on Quebec during which Montgomery was killed (December 31, 1775). When British ships appeared in the spring, the American retreat began, enabling Carleton to recover all of Canada in the summer of 1776 and

advance as far as Crown Point before returning to St. Johns to winter. Meanwhile, a feeble attempt by Americans and their sympathizers to capture Fort Cumberland (Beauséjour) in November, 1776, was repulsed without difficulty. In 1777, Burgoyne's campaign down the Lake Champlain route ended in his disastrous surrender at Saratoga (October 17) when Howe, instead of advancing to his support up the Hudson from New York, turned southward to capture Philadelphia and when St. Leger and his Indian and militia allies were halted before Fort Schuyler (Stanwix). The following years saw little action in the north except for privateering in the Atlantic coast and raids in the Mohawk Valley intended to interfere with the supply of food to Washington's army.

44 Fort Cumberland

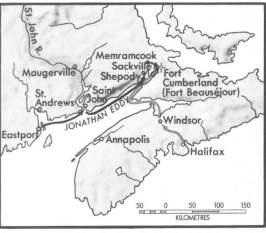

45   The Treaties of Versailles and Paris, 1783

Several treaties signed simultaneously on September 3, 1783, ended the American Revolutionary War and the world-wide conflicts that had arisen from it. Two concerned British North America:

The Treaty of Versailles between Britain and France altered the provisions of the Treaty of Paris (1763) by making France's ownership of St. Pierre and Miquelon unconditional and by adjusting French fishing rights on the northward and eastern shores of Newfoundland to make them lie between Cape St. John and Cape Ray instead of Cape Bonavista and Riche Point. In a special 'Declaration' that formed part of the agreement, the British Government undertook additionally to prevent its subjects from establishing fixed settlements along the 'French shore', thus virtually eliminating British use of almost half the island.

The Treaty of Paris between Britain and the United States. defining the new relationship of each to the other, included provision that the boundary between the United States and continuing British colonies to the north should run from the Bay of Fundy up the middle of the St. Croix River to its source, due north to the watershed between the St. Lawrence and the Atlantic, along the watershed to the north-westernmost head of the Connecticut River, down this to the 45th parallel, west along the parallel to the St. Lawrence, up the middle of that and other rivers and lakes to Lake Superior, Rainy Lake, and the Lake of the Woods, across the latter to its most north-western point, and finally due west to the Mississippi. In general this line was to constitute the per

H.M. Schooner *Tecumseth* built on Chippawa Creek, 1815

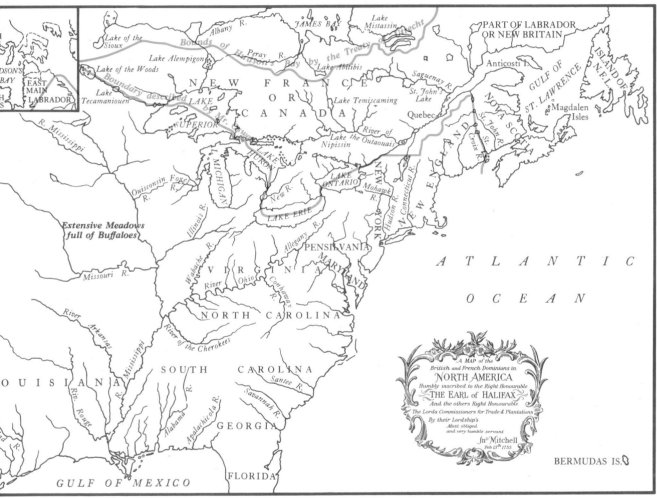

A MAP of the
British and French Dominions in
NORTH AMERICA
Humbly inscribed to the Right Honourable
THE EARL of HALIFAX
And the others Right Honourable
The Lords Commissioners for Trade & Plantations
By their Lordship's
Most obliged
and very humble servant
Jn.° Mitchell
Feb 13.th 1755

46 Mitchell's Map

manant boundary settlement, but several sections became subjects of controversy when the inadequacies of Mitchell's Map were discovered. In an attempt to remove these and other sources of discord, such as Britain's retention of important military and fur trading posts on American territory, Jay's Treaty was signed November 19, 1794. Its results included British withdrawal from the posts during 1796 and a decision by a joint commission as to which was meant by the St. Croix River. Other boundary problems remained for later solution.

Peace negotiators at Paris, bringing an end to the American Revolutionary War and defining the boundaries of the new United States, relied heavily on a map prepared for the British Government in 1755 by John Mitchell. A number of boundary problems were to arise from the fact, revealed by later exploration, that Mitchell's map contained important inaccuracies.

Newfoundland was highly important during the mercantile period because of its fishery, and the population increased to about 20 000 by the end of the eighteenth century in spite of earlier official attempts to prevent permanent settlement. Nova Scotia, British since 1713, attracted few new settlers before the founding of Halifax in 1749 when several thousand were brought out from England. Germans and some French and Swiss followed shortly, moving down the coast to Lunenburg. The conquest of France's remaining territories in North America and their retention by the Treaty of 1763 brought British merchants and garrisons to Quebec and Montreal, and groups of farmers migrated

from New England and directly from Britain to various places in the Maritimes.

However, it was the coming of the Loyalists, the refugees of the American Revolutionary War, that first foreshadowed an eventual British majority over the French in British North America. Estimates are that almost 20 000 settled finally in Nova Scotia, 14 000 in New Brunswick, 600 in Isle St. John, 400 in Cape Breton Island, 1000 in Lower Canada and 6000 in Upper Canada. The Maritimes group came mainly by ship from New York in 1783, many landing at Port Roseway (renamed Shelburne), temporarily the largest urban centre in British North America. Most soon went on to Halifax,

the Annapolis Valley, or across the Bay of Fundy to the St. John River Valley and its tributaries. Among the latter were several disbanded Loyalist corps and two Scottish regiments. The Quebec Loyalists, arriving more gradually by land, were forbidden by Haldimand, the governor, to settle in the vacant triangle beside the American border (later the Eastern Townships) or in the old French seigneuries except in the immediate vicinity of the refugee camp at William Henry (Sorel). Civilians and some military units spread out therefore along the waterfront from Lake St. Francis to beyond Cataraqui (Kingston). Farther west Joseph Brant's Iroquois received land along the

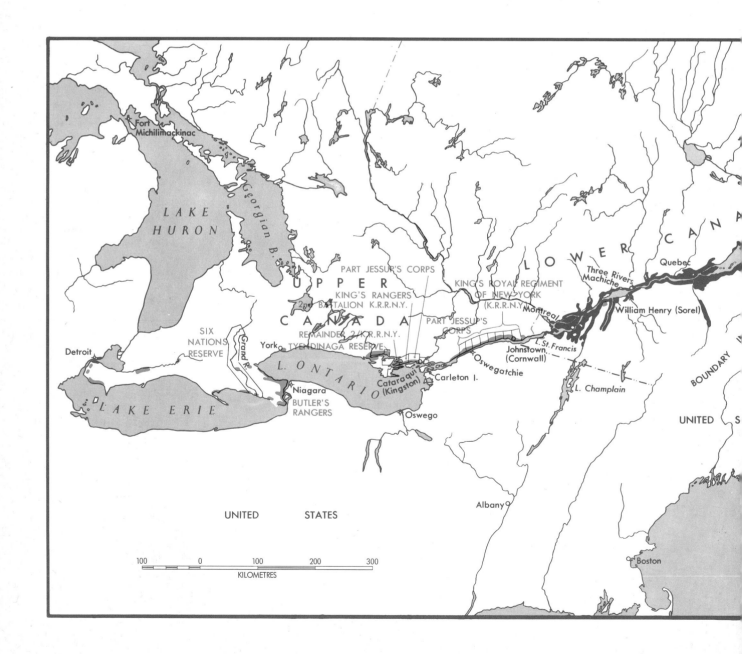

48 Military Settlements in New Brunswick

Grand River; Butler's Rangers stayed at Niagara where they had been based during the war. Other arrivals came from Detroit after the abandonment of that fort in 1796 under the terms of Jay's Treaty. In Canada, Loyalists were soon outnumbered by others moving westward with the frontier heedless of political boundaries; in the Maritimes, they remained dominant in the population for several generations.

The coming of the Loyalists coincided with and helped to cause the separation of New Brunswick and Cape Breton from Nova Scotia in 1784 and the division of Upper and Lower Canada following the Constitutional Act in 1791.

CHANGING RELATIONSHIPS,
1763–1822

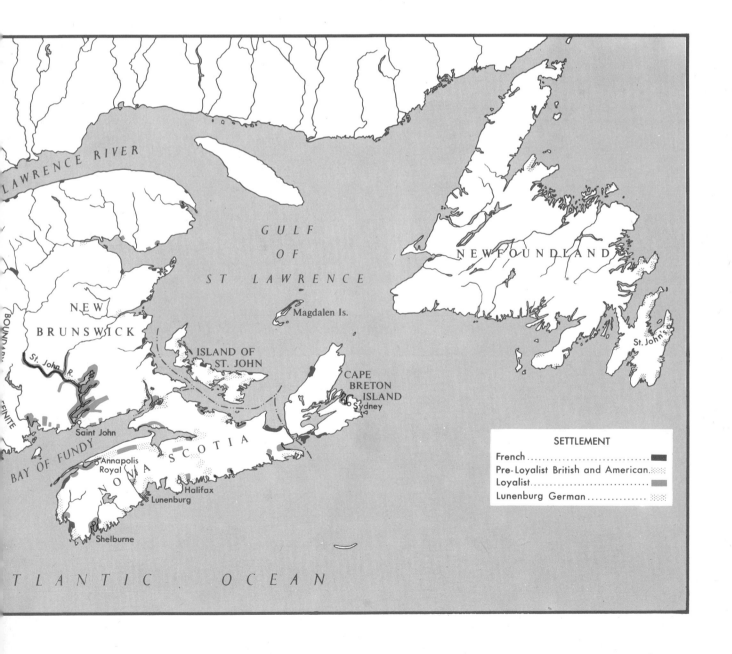

LAKE SUPERIOR

St. Joseph's I.

Michilimackinac
17 July 1812

LAKE HURON

Georgian Bay

Penetanguis
L. Sin

LAKE MICHIGAN

UPPER

Mississippi R.

Prairie du Chien
18 July 1814

York

Fort George

Stoney Creek
Queenston Heights
13 Oct. 1812

Moraviantown
5 Oct. 1813

Fort Dearborn
9 Aug. 1812
CAPTURED BY INDIANS

St. Louis

R.

Illinois R.

Wabash R.

Detroit
16 Aug. 1812

Amherstburg

LAKE ERIE

Erie
(Presqu'Isle)

Frenchtown

Put-in-Bay I.
10 Sept. 1813

Fort Meigs

To Urbana

Allegheny R.

Pittsburgh

Base map copyright Canadian Aero Service Limited, Ottawa

50 The Niagara Theatre

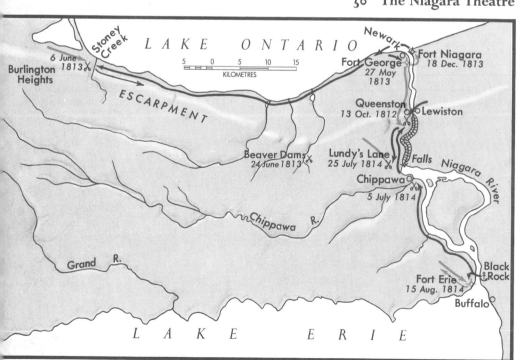

Stoney Creek

LAKE ONTARIO

Newark

6 June
1813

Burlington
Heights

ESCARPMENT

Fort Niagara
18 Dec. 1813

Fort George
27 May
1813

5   0   5   10   15
KILOMETRES

Queenston
13 Oct. 1812

Lewiston

Beaver Dams
24 June 1813

Lundy's Lane
25 July 1814

Falls

Niagara River

Chippawa
5 July 1814

Chippawa R.

Grand R.

Fort Erie
15 Aug. 1814

Black
Rock

Buffalo

LAKE ERIE

49 The War of 1812

The War of 1812, although related to the wider Napoleonic Wars and the earlier Revolutionary War and conducted partly by naval forces along the American seaboard, was primarily an American attempt to annex at least the western peninsula of Upper Canada. The main fighting, therefore, was around Niagara or farther west, and the Americans failed to concentrate on the traditional 'warpath of nations' along Lake Champlain where the capture of Montreal would have cut communications with Upper Canada and been a mortal blow. Their limited real objective also meant that the Americans fought half-heartedly at first, though with growing skill and determination as bloodshed increased, and it was possible to repel their invasion with what British troops were available aided by some militia units and Indians. Waterways being essential to communications, naval flotillas on the various lakes played a decisive role.

The main events year by year were: 1812. Shortly after the United States declared war (June 18), General Hull crossed the Detroit frontier into Canada (July 11), but retreated again when audacious British and Indian actions at Michilimackinac (July 17) and Fort Dearborn (August 9) gave

38

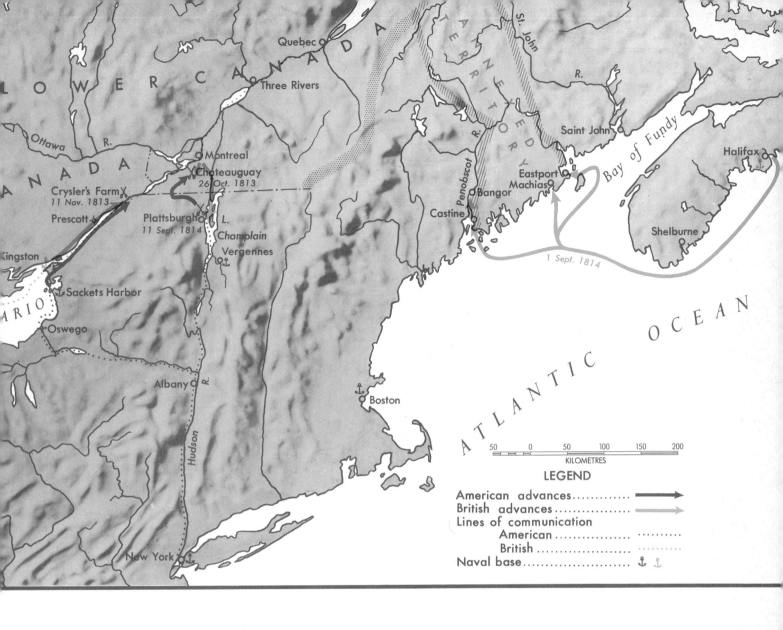

the British control of important Indian and fur-trading territories in his rear and when expected support from American settlers in Upper Canada was not forthcoming. Isaac Brock, following on his heels, captured Detroit itself (August 16) before turning back to bring about the defeat, at the cost of his own life, of a more energetic American crossing in the Niagara region at Queenston Heights (October 13).

1813. In a second Niagara effort, the Americans captured Fort George (May 27), but their farther advance was halted at Stoney Creek (June 5-6) by a daring night attack under John Harvey, and before the year's end Fort George had been abandoned and the American side of the Niagara River was being devastated by British raiders. Westward, however, a small but decisive naval engagement at Put-in-Bay (September 10) gave the Americans permanent command of Lake Erie and forced a British withdrawal towards Niagara in the course of which, in the Battle of the Thames River near Moraviantown (October 5), the great Indian leader, Tecumseh, was slain. On the other hand, in the east, a two-pronged attack on Montreal from Lake Champlain and Lake Ontario was effectively parried at Chateau-

guay (October 26) and Crysler's Farm (November 11).

1814. At Niagara, where the main fighting now centred, the Americans captured Fort Erie (July 3), went on to a victory at Chippawa (July 5), but were turned back after a major engagement at Lundy's Lane (July 25). Although successful in beating off a heavy assault on Fort Erie (August 15) they had eventually to abandon it also (November 5) before winter set in. Meanwhile, Napoleon's defeat and abdication (April 11) had released some of Wellington's veterans for Canadian service, and Prevost, the governor-in-chief and commander of the forces, led a powerful invading force across the Lake Champlain frontier (September 1). His ineptness and a premature naval battle at Plattsburgh (September 11), which gave command of Lake Champlain to the Americans, obliged him to retreat ignominiously. The more successful lieutenant-governor of Nova Scotia, Sir John Sherbrooke, was at the same time annexing most of the district of Maine (September 1-21) while in the far west Britain's hold on the Indian territories had been strengthened by the capture of Prairie du Chien (July 18) and the successful defence of Michilimackinac (August 4).

51 The Montreal Region

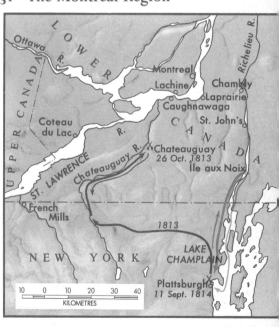

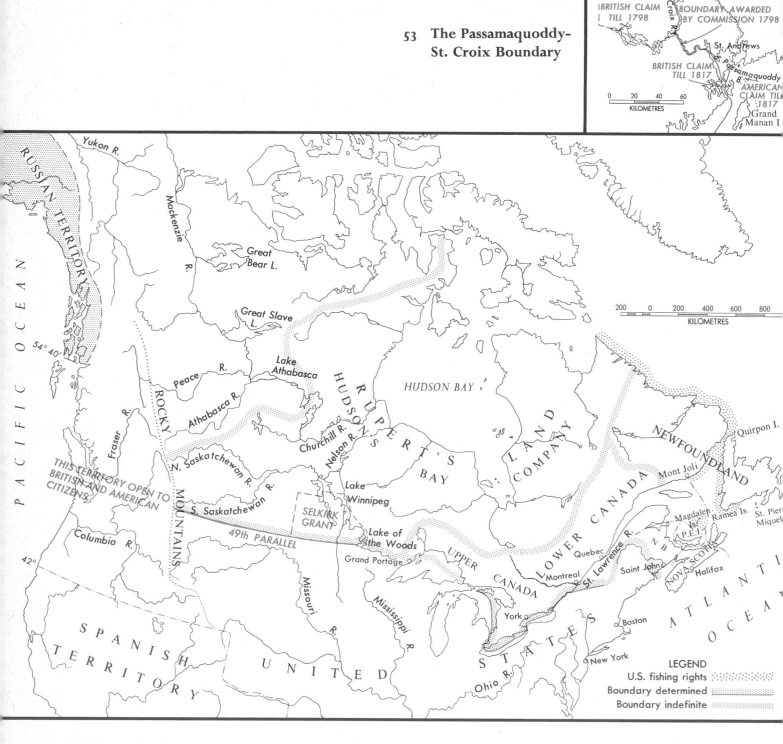

52 The Peace Settlements, 1814–22

The Treaty of Ghent (December 24, 1814) dealt with none of the problems alleged as causes of war in 1812, but simply restored peace and the 1783 boundary. Its most important provisions were for several commissions to define that boundary more accurately (1) where it divided the islands of Passamaquoddy Bay, (2) in the St. Croix and Connecticut River Region, (3) from the St. Lawrence through to the waterways leading into Lake Superior, (4) through these and Lake Superior and to the north-western point of the Lake of the Woods. The first and third commissions achieved permanent settlements in reports dated November 24, 1817, and June 18, 1822, respectively. The

other two ended in disagreement and final decisions on these sections were not reached until the Webster-Ashburton Treaty of 1842 (see Map 71).

Meanwhile, notes exchanged between the British minister in Washington, Sir Charles Bagot (April 28, 1817) and the acting American secretary of state, Richard Rush (April 29, 1817) resulted in an 'Arrangement' proclaimed by President Monroe (April 28, 1818) for naval disarmament on the Lakes, each side keeping the right to only one vessel on Lake Ontario, two on the Upper Lakes, and one on Lake Champlain, none to exceed 100 tons or carry more than one 18-pounder gun. A further Convention

of Commerce between the two countries (October 20, 1818) granted Americans certain fishing rights round the Magdalen Islands, on the coasts of Newfoundland from the Ramea Islands around Cape Ray to Quirpon Island, and on Labrador (transferred back from Lower Canada to Newfoundland in 1809) from Mont Joli through the Strait of Belle Isle northward indefinitely to the Hudson's Bay Company's territories. It provided also that the British-American boundary west of the Lake of the Woods should follow the 49th parallel to the 'Stony Mountains' and that west of the mountains the territories claimed by each should be open to both for ten years.

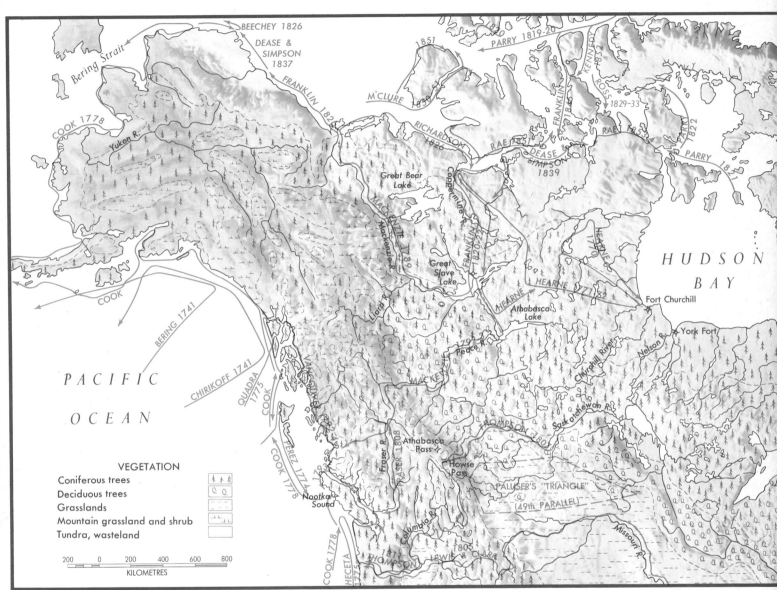

Base map copyright Canadian Aero Service Limited, Ottawa

54 The Explorers

Urged on by fur-trading and national rivalries, the exploration of the prairie, Arctic, and Pacific regions continued steadily in the century after the British conquest of Canada. The Montreal 'pedlars', banded together in the North West Company, forced the pace into newer and richer fur-trading areas and produced such great explorers as Alexander Mackenzie, Simon Fraser, and David Thompson. Hudson's Bay Company interests were furthered by Samuel Hearne and others. Governments also, well before the end of the eighteenth century, had begun to participate in exploration on grounds of national and scientific as well as commercial interest. A major role, for example, was played on the Pacific Coast by such official expeditions as those of the Russians Bering and Chirikoff, the Spaniards Pérez, Heceta, and Quadra, the Britons Cook and Vancouver, and the Americans Lewis and Clark. Similarly knowledge of the western Arctic was rounded out mainly by government-supported British expeditions including those of Parry, Franklin, Richardson, Beechey, and Rae. The Hudson's Bay Company sponsored Dease and Simpson. The many expeditions sent out in search of Franklin when he failed to return from his 1845 voyage were of special importance in adding to knowledge of the northern archipelago. Palliser and others were engaged by the British or Canadian Governments to carry out the scientific examinations of the prairies necessary to enable the homesteaders to take over from the buffalo hunters.

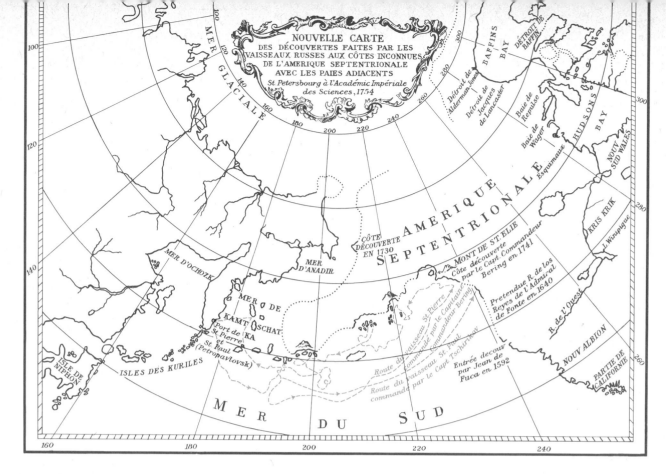

55   Muller's Map, 1754

Two eighteenth-century maps, one drawn in Russia and the other in the United States, make clear the international character of Pacific Coast exploration at that time. The map prepared in St. Petersburg for the Imperial Academy of Sciences, was published in G. F. Muller's *History of Russia*. The map of Captain Cook's British expedition was published by a young American, John Ledyard, who had served with Cook.

56   Ledyard's Map, 1783

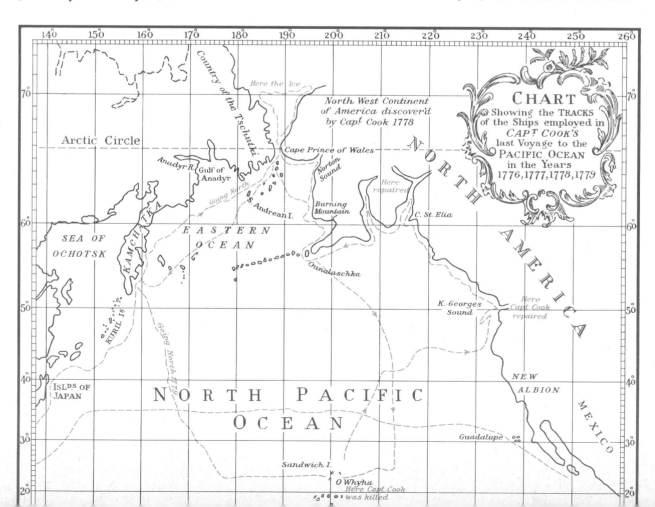

57 Oregon and British Columbia

National claims on the Pacific Coast began to be delimited when: (1) Spain abandoned all claim to the coast north of the 42nd parallel in the Treaty of Florida Blanca with the United States (February 22, 1819); and (2) Russia abandoned all claim to the coast south of the 54° 40′ parallel in treaties with the United States (April 17, 1824) and Britain (February 22, 1825). The treaty with Britain also provided that the inland boundary of Russian territory should be the first range of mountains and the 141st meridian. Meanwhile Britain and the United States had agreed in their 'Convention of Commerce' (October 20, 1818) that territories west of the mountains claimed by each should be open to the citizens of both for a ten-year period. Later renewed (October 6, 1827), this agreement broke down in the 1840's and faced with the possibility of war the two nations signed the Oregon Treaty (June 15, 1846), extending their joint boundary westward along the 49th parallel to the coast and thence through the main channel between the mainland and Vancouver Island. A later dispute as to which was the intended channel was referred in the Treaty of Washington (May 8, 1871) to the German Emperor for arbitration. His award (October 21, 1872) was in line with the American claim.

British governmental organization took shape as follows: (1) Vancouver Island was granted to the Hudson's Bay Company (January 13, 1849) on condition of establishing a colony. Its lieutenant-governor was given authority to administer the Queen Charlotte Islands (July 9, 1852) after the discovery of gold there. The colony reverted to the Crown when Hudson's Bay Company rights were revoked (May 30, 1858). (2) The Gold Rush to the Fraser Valley led to the creation of a separate crown colony of British Columbia (August 20, 1858) to which the Queen Charlotte Islands were now attached. (3) Discovery of gold in the Stikine Valley was followed by the organization of the Stikine Territory (1862) under the administration of the governor of British Columbia and its incorporation into British Columbia the following year but with somewhat altered boundaries. (4) The colonies of British Columbia and Vancouver Island were united (November 17, 1866). Meanwhile road building, largely by a party of Royal Engineers, had opened the way to the main mining centres.

THE ARCTIC, THE PLAINS,
AND THE PACIFIC

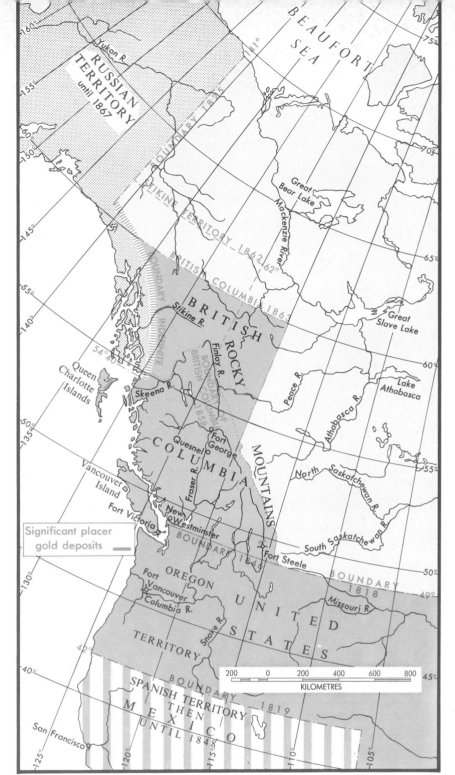

Significant placer gold deposits —

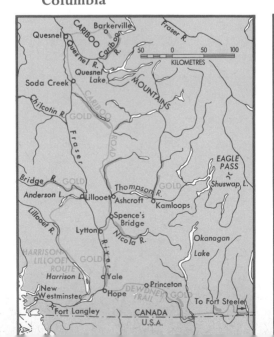

58 The Interior of British Columbia

59 The San Juan Boundary Dispute

A *canot de maitre*

61 The Red River Settlement

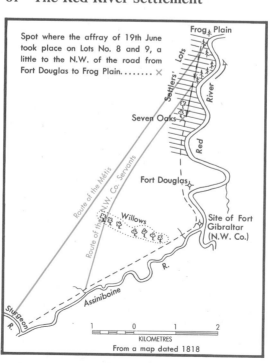

Spot where the affray of 19th June took place on Lots No. 8 and 9, a little to the N.W. of the road from Fort Douglas to Frog Plain. . . . . ✕

Frog Plain

Settlers' Lots

Red River

Seven Oaks

Route of the Métis

Route of the N.W. Co. Servants

Fort Douglas

Willows

Site of Fort Gibraltar (N.W. Co.)

Assiniboine R.

Sturgeon R.

KILOMETRES

From a map dated 1818

60 Fur-trade Rivalries to 1821

Basic in the great fur trade of the north-west were: (1) The forest belt from Lake Winnipeg to the Rockies and from the North Saskatchewan to the Arctic barrens. This was the western and widest section of the huge transcontinental northern or boreal forest, the home of the beaver and other fur-bearing animals with pelts made finer by cold winters; (2) the complex of interlocking waterways suitable for canoe transportation. The three main river systems were the Saskatchewan, draining into Lake Winnipeg and thence to Hudson Bay, the Churchill flowing directly into the Bay, and the Mackenzie into the Arctic. Two portages of key importance linking these were Frog Portage (Portage de Traite) on the most used route between the Saskatchewan and Churchill basins, and Methye Portage (Portage La Loche) between the Churchill and the Mackenzie.

Access to the region for the Montrealers of the North West Company, after they had completed their long passage to the western end of Lake Superior, was by Grand Portage until 1803. Then, because this route lay in American territory, it was abandoned in favour of one up the Kaministiquia River, at the mouth of which Fort William was built as the Nor'Westers' inland headquarters. The Hudson's Bay Company was more fortunate in having direct entry through York Fort or alternatively Fort Churchill (Fort Prince of Wales) or even Fort Albany. Rival posts at strategic places in the interior were rapidly established by both companies and at some agriculture was encouraged to supply the trappers and traders. Increasingly violent competition led to bloodshed after 1811 when the Hudson's Bay Company granted Lord Selkirk Assiniboia with its agricultural possibilities and its threat to the Nor'Westers' main communication line. Only with the amalgamation of the two companies ten years later was peace restored. The enlarged Hudson's Bay Company kept its ancient charter territory of Rupert's Land and received under terms of a twenty-one year licence from the British Government other lands to the west. These included, in addition to the Mackenzie River basin, the Rocky Mountain and Pacific Coast regions. In the latter, important for its rich trade with Canton in sea otter and other furs, the Americans had equal rights prior to the Oregon Treaty and the Hudson's Bay Company had to compete with both American and Russian fur traders.

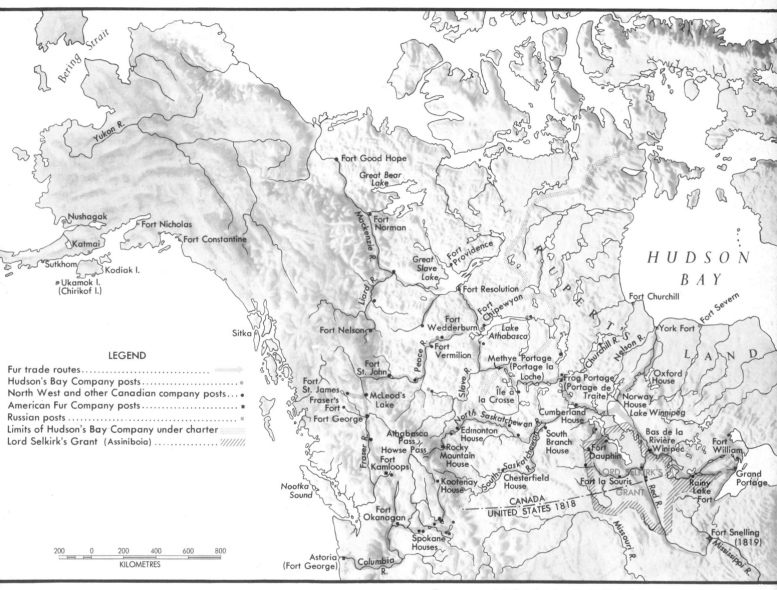

LEGEND

Fur trade routes..................................
Hudson's Bay Company posts........................ •
North West and other Canadian company posts... •
American Fur Company posts....................... ■
Russian posts................................... ■
Limits of Hudson's Bay Company under charter ░░░
Lord Selkirk's Grant (Assiniboia) .... ▨

200   0   200   400   600   800
KILOMETRES

HUDSON BAY

RUPERT'S LAND

CANADA
UNITED STATES 1818

Base map copyright Canadian Aero Service Limited, Ottawa

The Grand Portage and Kaministiquia Routes

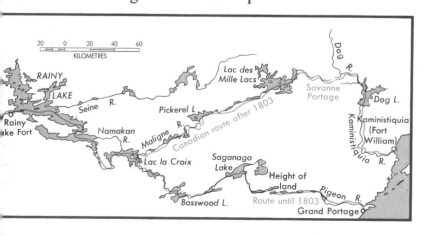

20   0   20   40   60
KILOMETRES

RAINY LAKE
Rainy Lake Fort
Seine R.
Namakan R.
Lac la Croix
Maligne R.
Pickerel L.
Lac des Mille Lacs
Canadian route after 1803
Savanne Portage
Dog R.
Dog L.
Kaministiquia (Fort William)
Kaministiquia R.
Saganaga Lake
Height of land
Basswood L.
Route until 1803
Pigeon R.
Grand Portage

Hudson's Bay Company.   A York boat

45

FURS TO BRITAIN

Fort Churchill

H U D S O N

B A Y

York Factory

FURS

FURS

FURS

Fort Severn

Lake
Winnipeg

FURS

FURS

Fort
Garry

Fort
Albany

Rupert House

Moose Factory

FURS

FURS, WHEAT
MANUFACTURED GOODS

FROM
c. 1850

Fort William

FURS

TILL

1821

St. Paul

Mississippi
River

FURS AND TIMBER

TIMBER

ST. LAWRENCE RIVER

Rivière
du-Lo

Quebec

LUMBER FROM 1854

TIMBER

FOODSTUFFS

FROM CANADA
TIMBER AND
FOODSTUFFS
FROM 1853

Bytown
(Ottawa)
Rideau Canal
TIMBER AND
FOODSTUFFS

Montreal

Chicago

Detroit

York
(Toronto)

Kingston

Portland

TIMBER AND
FOODSTUFFS

Buffalo

ERIE

Oswego

1841

Mohawk R.

1839

Boston

U.S. GRAIN TO
ST. LAWRENCE PORTS
FROM BEFORE 1850

Dunkirk

CANAL

1825

1851

Hudson R.

From Canada: Timber
To Canada: Foodstuffs

CANADIAN AND U.S.
PRODUCE TO NEW
YORK FROM 1825

New York

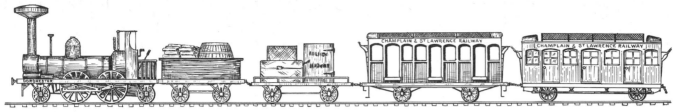

Canada's first train

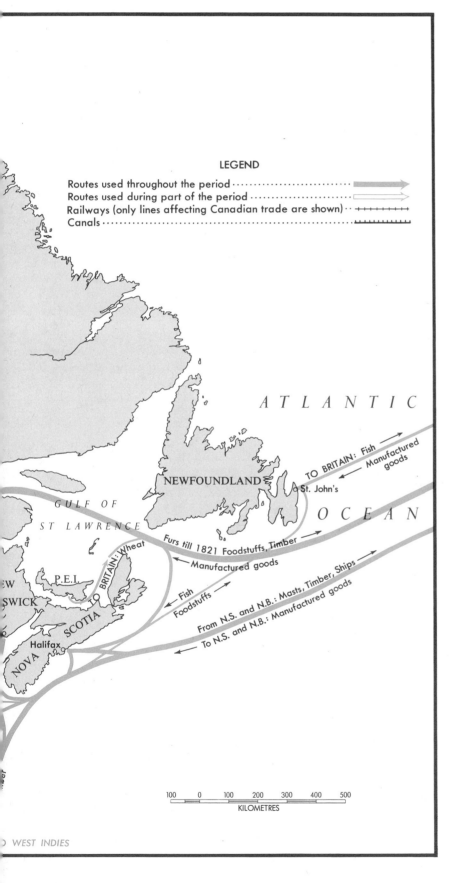

LEGEND

Routes used throughout the period ····························· ⟶
Routes used during part of the period ······················· ⟶
Railways (only lines affecting Canadian trade are shown) ·· ++++++++
Canals ··

ATLANTIC

TO BRITAIN: Fish ⟶
Manufactured goods ⟵

NEWFOUNDLAND
○ St. John's

OCEAN

GULF OF
ST LAWRENCE

Furs till 1821 Foodstuffs, Timber ⟶
⟵ Manufactured goods

P.E.I.

TO BRITAIN: Wheat

EW

SWICK

SCOTIA

NOVA

Halifax

Fish ⟵
Foodstuffs ⟵

From N.S. and N.B.: Masts, Timber, Ships ⟶
To N.S. and N.B.: Manufactured goods ⟵

100   0   100   200   300   400   500
KILOMETRES

WEST INDIES

63   The Commercial Empire of the St. Lawrence

The British North American Provinces (including Newfoundland) grew in population from not quite half a million early in the nineteenth century to about three and a half million in 1861, the time of the last census in most of them before Confederation. Economic changes were correspondingly great. Early dependence on the fur trade and the fisheries was replaced by greater emphasis on the export of timber and grain and by the gradual development of secondary industries such as lumber and flour milling and shipbuilding. The construction of roads, canals, and railways became essential and proceeded apace, although less rapidly than in the United States. The relationship of the St. Lawrence to its old commercial rivals, Hudson Bay and the Hudson River, changed too. It lost to Hudson Bay the whole fur trade of the north-west after the amalgamation of the North West and the Hudson's Bay Companies in 1821. Although its total trade continued to grow, with growing exports of timber and grain, the St. Lawrence fell gradually further behind the Hudson River of which the natural advantages were enhanced by the opening of the Erie Canal in 1825 and by rapidly extending railways into the interior.

THE CANADAS, 1791–1867

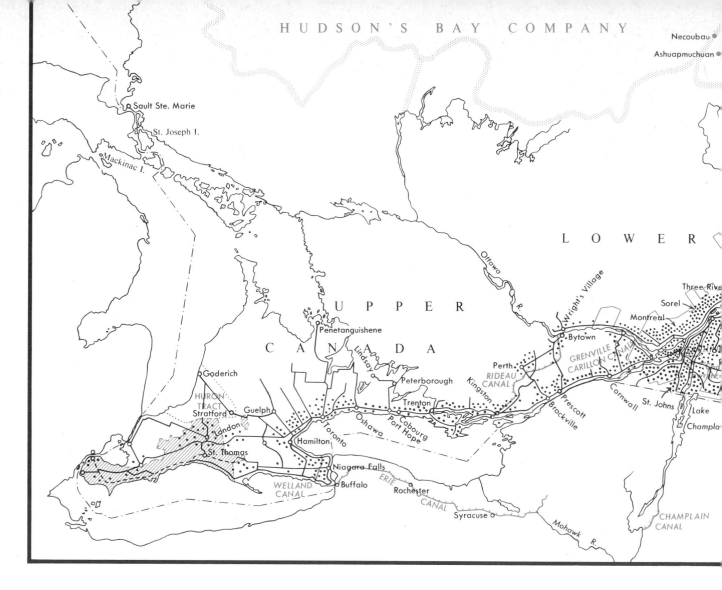

L O W E R

U P P E R   C A N A D A

Necoubau
Ashuapmuchuan

Sault Ste. Marie
St. Joseph I.
Mackinac I.

Penetanguishene

Goderich
HURON TRACT
Guelph
Stratford
London
St. Thomas
Hamilton
Toronto
Niagara Falls
Buffalo
Rochester
WELLAND CANAL
ERIE CANAL
Syracuse
Mohawk R.

Lindsay
Peterborough
Trenton
Cobourg
Port Hope
Oshawa

Ottawa R.
Wright's Village
Bytown
Perth
RIDEAU CANAL
Kingston
GRENVILLE CARILLON CANAL
Prescott
Brockville
Cornwall
St. Johns

Three Rive
Sorel
Montreal

Lake Champla

CHAMPLAIN CANAL

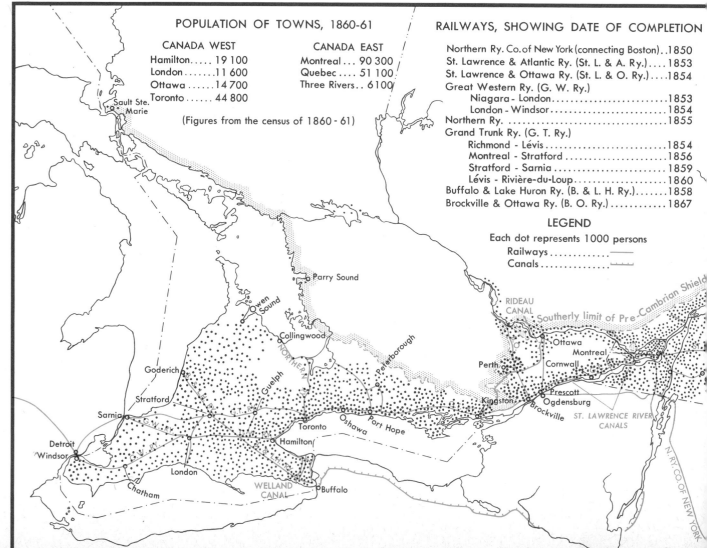

POPULATION OF TOWNS, 1860-61

CANADA WEST

Hamilton	19 100
London	11 600
Ottawa	14 700
Toronto	44 800

CANADA EAST

Montreal	90 300
Quebec	51 100
Three Rivers	6100

(Figures from the census of 1860 - 61)

RAILWAYS, SHOWING DATE OF COMPLETION

Northern Ry. Co. of New York (connecting Boston)	1850
St. Lawrence & Atlantic Ry. (St. L. & A. Ry.)	1853
St. Lawrence & Ottawa Ry. (St. L. & O. Ry.)	1854
Great Western Ry. (G. W. Ry.)	
Niagara - London	1853
London - Windsor	1854
Northern Ry.	1855
Grand Trunk Ry. (G. T. Ry.)	
Richmond - Lévis	1854
Montreal - Stratford	1856
Stratford - Sarnia	1859
Lévis - Rivière-du-Loup	1860
Buffalo & Lake Huron Ry. (B. & L. H. Ry.)	1858
Brockville & Ottawa Ry. (B. O. Ry.)	1867

LEGEND

Each dot represents 1000 persons

Railways ....

Canals ....

Sault Ste. Marie

Parry Sound

Owen Sound

Collingwood

NORTHERN

Goderich
Guelph
Stratford
Sarnia
G.W.Ry.
Detroit
Windsor
London
Chatham
WELLAND CANAL
Buffalo
Toronto
Hamilton
Oshawa
Port Hope
Peterborough

RIDEAU CANAL
Southerly limit of Pre-Cambrian Shield
Ottawa
Montreal
Perth
Cornwall
Kingston
Ogdensburg
Prescott
Brockville
ST. LAWRENCE RIVER CANALS

N. RY. CO. OF NEW YORK

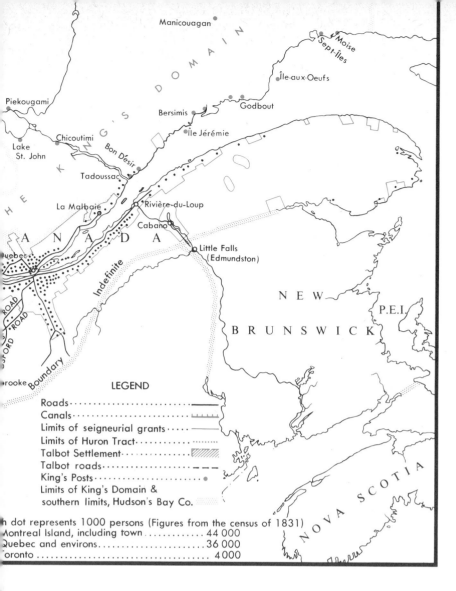

LEGEND

Roads ....
Canals ....
Limits of seigneurial grants .....
Limits of Huron Tract ....
Talbot Settlement ....
Talbot roads ....
King's Posts ....
Limits of King's Domain &
southern limits, Hudson's Bay Co.

h dot represents 1000 persons (Figures from the census of 1831)
Aontreal Island, including town 44 000
Quebec and environs........................ 36 000
oronto 4 000

64 Settlement and Communications to 1840

Upper Canada attracted immigration after it became a separate province in 1791 and newcomers soon greatly outnumbered the original Loyalists. Before the War of 1812 most were Americans, but the influx afterwards, which included some disbanded troops, was mainly from the British Isles. Lower Canada with its outdated seigneuries, not abolished until 1854, progressed more slowly except in the freehold Eastern Townships.

Settlement was assisted to some extent by governments but also by land companies, emigration societies, and private individuals such as Thomas Talbot. It was handicapped at first by the clergy- and crown-reserves policy of the British Government and by corruption and inefficiency in land administration.

Early improvements in communications, so vital to settlement, took the form of road and canal building and after 1809 the rapid growth of steamship services. In the 1830's railroads began to be projected but prior to the Act of Union of 1840 only the 25-km Champlain and St. Lawrence line had actually come into operation. The next decades saw the completion and improvement of the canal systems and, in particular, quite extensive railway building totalling almost 3200 km by 1860.

With these changes the old fur trade, except at the King's Posts (leased by the Hudson's Bay Company, 1842–59), gave way to agriculture, lumbering, shipbuilding, etc.

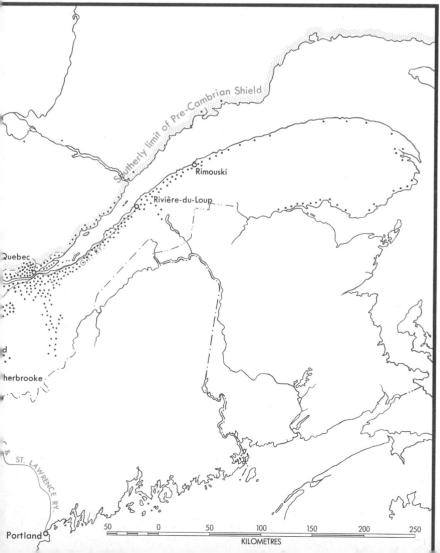

65 Settlement and Communications, 1841–67

66 A Township with 'Chequer Board' Reserves

The township was the unit of settlement during the British period as the seigneury had been during the French. The typical township was 16 kilometres square or, if on navigable water, 19 km in depth with a 14 km water frontage. Modifications due to local circumstances were very frequent, however. The Constitutional Act of 1791 provided that lands 'equal in value to the Seventh Part' of grants made since the beginning of British rule, and subsequently of all future grants, should be reserved in both Upper and Lower Canada for use of the Protestant clergy, and Colonial Office instructions reserved another seventh for the Crown. The 'chequer board' pattern of these reserves was intended to scatter them evenly throughout each township but it was often departed from. Being held for later and more profitable sale the reserves began to impede settlement by about 1820. The crown reserves in Upper Canada (560 244 ha) together with the Huron Tract (404 680 ha) were eventually disposed of to the Canada Company in 1825. A similar arrangement regarding the crown reserves in lower Canada (101 711 ha) and other unsurveyed land (241 321 ha) was made in 1834 with the British American Land Company. Gradual sale of the clergy reserves was authorized in 1827 and the final secularization of those remaining took place in 1854.

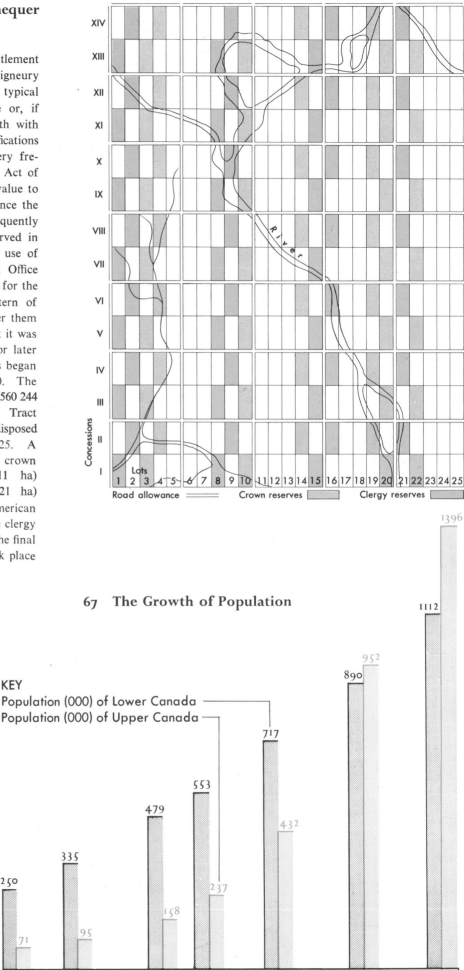

67   The Growth of Population

KEY
Population (000) of Lower Canada
Population (000) of Upper Canada

	1806	1814	1825	1831	1840	1851	1861
Lower Canada	250	335	479	553	717	890	1112
Upper Canada	71	95	158	237	432	952	1396

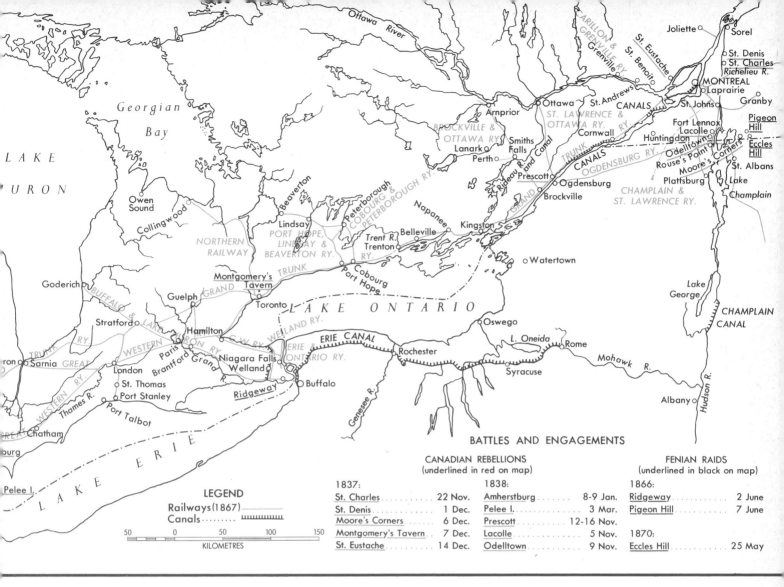

BATTLES AND ENGAGEMENTS

CANADIAN REBELLIONS
(underlined in red on map)

FENIAN RAIDS
(underlined in black on map)

1837:

St. Charles	22 Nov.
St. Denis	1 Dec.
Moore's Corners	6 Dec.
Montgomery's Tavern	7 Dec.
St. Eustache	14 Dec.

1838:

Amherstburg	8-9 Jan.
Pelee I.	3 Mar.
Prescott	12-16 Nov.
Lacolle	5 Nov.
Odelltown	9 Nov.

1866:

| Ridgeway | 2 June |
| Pigeon Hill | 7 June |

1870:

| Eccles Hill | 25 May |

LEGEND

Railways (1867) _____
Canals .... ⊔⊔⊔⊔⊔⊔⊔

50 0 50 100 150
KILOMETRES

68 The Canadian Rebellions, 1837–8

Political and other grievances, made more bitter in Lower Canada by ethnic division, led to armed violence beginning with rioting in Montreal in November, 1837. During the next month or so there were serious clashes, the chief centres of disaffection being the Richelieu parishes and the Lake of Two Mountains area. After an initial check at St. Denis, regular troops and volunteers suppressed the disturbances, the final and most bloody encounter being at St. Eustache. In Upper Canada a farcical encounter between government supporters and rebels on Toronto's Yonge Street was followed by hasty flight on both sides. The following day (December 7) a city militia force dispersed the rebels at Montgomery's Tavern. Troubles were prolonged for a few months by rebels who escaped to the United States and with the aid of quite numerous American sympathizers undertook a variety of futile skirmishes across the border including a serious raid at Prescott which coincided with a brief second rebellion in Lower Canada.

The Fenian Raids, 1866–71

The Fenian Brotherhood, organized in Ireland and among Irish Americans to win Ireland's independence from Britain, took advantage of the general restlessness in the United States and hostility towards Britain following the American Civil War to make several raids on Canada. A half-hearted attempt on New Brunswick's Campobello Island was followed by a much more serious effort under John O'Neill who led 1500 Fenians across the Niagara River on May 31, 1866, and won a victory over a Canadian force at Ridgeway before withdrawing. Simultaneously there was some plundering on the border east of Lake Champlain and a minor raid was repulsed near Huntingdon. Despite many alarms, the only other major raid was in May, 1870, when a force raised by O'Neill was met by resolute Canadians at Eccles Hill and driven back across the border. An attempt on Manitoba in 1871 was broken up by American troops.

THE CANADAS, 1791–1867

The sea was fundamental to the economy of the Atlantic Colonies. It supplied them with their valuable inshore and bank fisheries and with access to the markets of Europe and the West Indies. Although all four colonies had much in common, each acquired distinctive characteristics. Newfoundland depended almost entirely on the cod fisheries. Nova Scotia had in addition a substantial

shipbuilding and shipping industry and some coal mining and agriculture. New Brunswick rivalled Nova Scotia in shipbuilding and shipping, exported a large amount of squared timber to Britain and miscellaneous lumber and staves to the West Indies, and carried on some fishing and agriculture. Agriculture was Prince Edward Island's main resource.

Settlement throughout the region was along the coast or up main river valleys. It was encouraged by the cheap though extremely hazardous and uncomfortable passages available to immigrants in returning timber ships. Even so it took place more slowly than in the Canadas.

Roads and stage coaches soon supplemented river and coastal shipping. This

69   A Maritime Economy

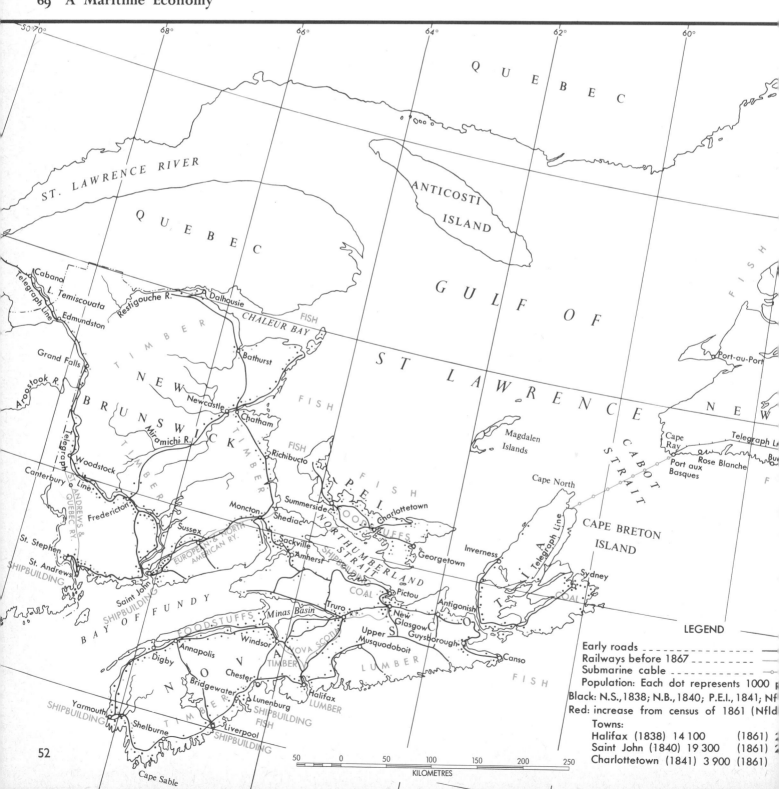

LEGEND

Early roads – – – –
Railways before 1867 – – – –
Submarine cable – – – –
Population: Each dot represents 1000 p
Black: N.S.,1838; N.B.,1840; P.E.I.,1841; Nf
Red: increase from census of 1861 (Nfld

Towns:
Halifax (1838) 14 100   (1861)
Saint John (1840) 19 300   (1861)
Charlottetown (1841) 3 900 (1861)

52

latter was greatly improved when steamships began to be introduced in the 1820's. The first regular trans-Atlantic steamship service was inaugurated by Samuel Cunard of Halifax in 1840. Railway construction by 1866 amounted to 351 km in New Brunswick and 237 km in Nova Scotia.

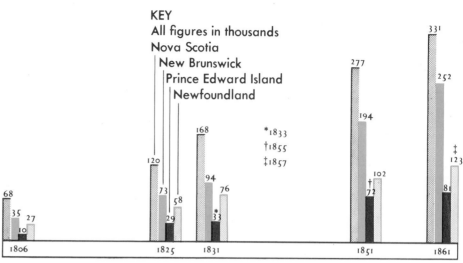

KEY
All figures in thousands
Nova Scotia
New Brunswick
Prince Edward Island
Newfoundland

*1833
†1855
‡1857

70 The Growth of Population

71 The Webster-Ashburton Boundary Settlement, 1842

Badly defined in the Treaty of Paris (1783) and despite further efforts under the terms of Jay's Treaty (1794) and the Treaty of Ghent (1814), the American border with New Brunswick and Canada remained undetermined when lumbermen from both sides began to enter the region in the 1820's. An American threat in 1828, firmly resisted by the New Brunswick authorities, led to a request for arbitration by the King of the Netherlands, but his Award (1831) was rejected by the United States. More serious local disturbances in 1839 followed by warlike threats and preparations by the governments concerned—the so-called Aroostook or 'Pork and Beans' War—made clear the need for a final settlement. This was achieved in the Webster-Ashburton Treaty (1842) which, although it left a wedge of Maine projecting between New Brunswick and Canada, kept intact the vital communication route from Fredericton to Quebec via Lake Temiscouata and was more favourable to Britain than the Award of 1831 had been.

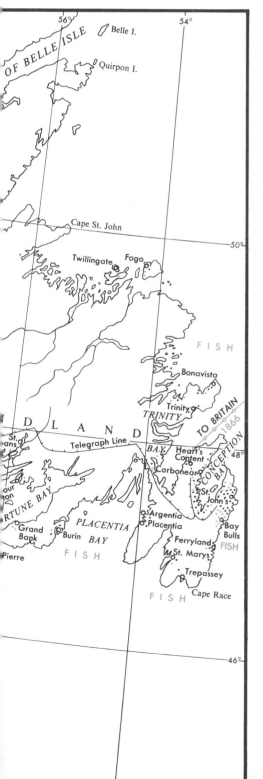

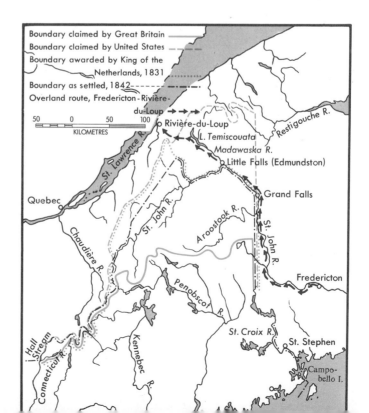

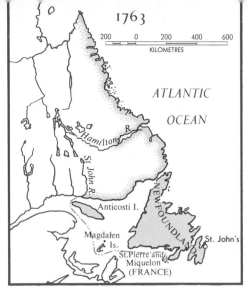

1763

1774

1809

1825

Newfoundland and Labrador

73   in 1763
74   in 1774
75   in 1809
76   in 1825

The fisheries constituted the key to Newfoundland's evolution in the century before 1867. They account for the fact that when France was obliged to give up all other Newfoundland claims in the Treaty of Utrecht (1713) she insisted on keeping fishing rights along what came to be known as the 'French Shore'. These rights were modified slightly in the Treaty of Versailles (1783), were lost during the French Revolutionary and Napoleonic Wars, and were renewed in the Treaty of Paris (1815). They denied British subjects effective use of a large part of Newfoundland's coastline until finally abrogated in 1904. The United States managed to obtain similar, but less extensive, rights along part of the coast in the Convention of Commerce (1818) and round all of it in the Reciprocity Treaty (1854–65).

Meanwhile Labrador and some adjacent islands passed back and forth several times between Newfoundland and Canada in response to pressure from rival fishing and other interests. Anticosti, the Magdalen Islands, and Labrador from the St. John River to Hudson Strait were first transferred from the newly acquired Canada to Newfoundland by Royal Proclamation (1763) and then returned to Canada by the Quebec Act (1774). Newfoundland got back all but the Magdalen Islands in the first Labrador Act (1809) but again lost Anticosti and the coast of Labrador as far east as Anse Sablon in the second Labrador Act (1825). Not until a decision by the Judicial Committee of the Privy Council in 1927 was the Labrador–Quebec boundary finally determined.

72 Newfoundland Fisheries

The British North America Act of March 29, 1867, provided for the confederation of the colonies of Canada (simultaneously to be divided into Ontario and Quebec), New Brunswick, and Nova Scotia, and for their being linked by an intercolonial railway. The Dominion of Canada came into existence accordingly on July 1, 1867, and the railway was formally opened on July 1, 1876. Meanwhile on July 15, 1870, after lengthy negotiations with the Hudson's Bay Company and the British Government, and after further delays due to the Red River Insurrection, the Hudson's Bay and Northwest Territories were transferred to Canada, part becoming the Province of Manitoba and the rest being placed under territorial government. A year later, on July 20, 1871, British Columbia entered Confederation on terms that included, among other things, the building of a transcontinental railway line.

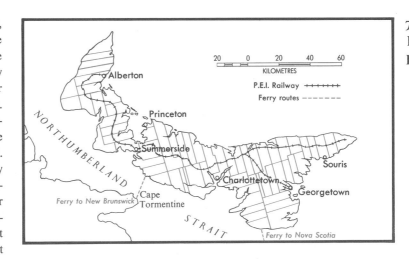

78 Prince Edward Island's Proprietors

The Canadian Pacific Railway built to meet this undertaking was completed November 7, 1885. Prince Edward Island joined Canada on July 1, 1873, on being promised the maintenance of continuous communications with the mainland, the taking over and completion of her railway, and aid in buying out her proprietors. These latter, many of them absentees, were the owners of the 67 lots into which the Island had been divided in 1767.

77 Rounding out Confederation

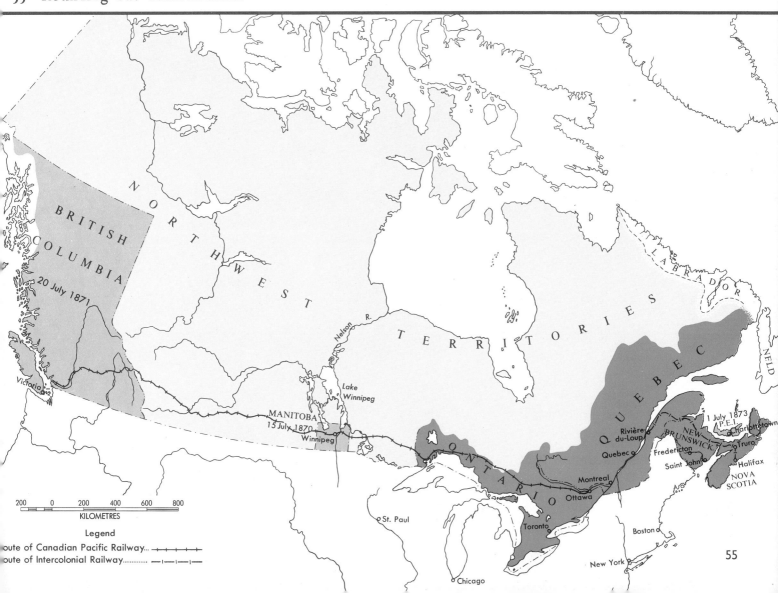

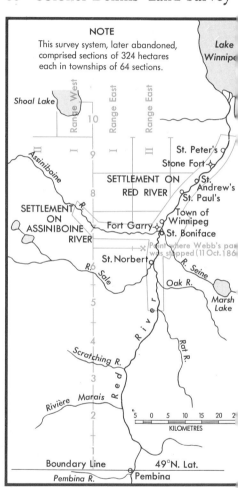

The Red River Insurrection, 1869–70

The opening of the West, with its repercussions on the rest of Canada as well, was among the most important features of Canadian history between Confederation and the First World War. The beginning was unfortunate. The Red River Insurrection occurred at the outset when negotiations for the transfer to Canada of the Hudson's Bay and Northwest Territories failed to take into sufficient account the interests and anxieties of their inhabitants. The great majority of these, apart from the scattered Indian tribes, lived in the Red River Settlement, most were semi-nomadic people of part Indian descent, mainly French-speaking and Roman

Catholic. The Métis' fears that an influx of settlers from Canada (probably English and Protestant) would follow the transfer were strengthened by two preliminary Canadian actions, the commencement in 1868 of a road forming the most westerly portion of the combined road and river route between Port Arthur and Fort Garry recommended in 1858 by S. J. Dawson, and the general land survey undertaken in the summer of 1869 by a party under Colonel J. S. Dennis. Dennis' survey, although based on the American system of square townships, was accompanied by a careful promise to respect claims to existing strip

farms running back from the Red and Assiniboine Rivers. That it provoked the Métis to physical resistance was because it seemed an assertion of Canadian authority over-riding any right of the inhabitants even to consultation. Full-scale insurrection followed with Louis Riel assuming the leadership.

Eventually after Canadian negotiations with Riel's provisional government had resulted in the passage of the Manitoba Act (May 12, 1870), the 37 141 km² province of Manitoba and the Northwest Territories became part of Canada (July 15, 1870). To ensure against further disorders and

81 Indian Treaties

atisfy public opinion in Ontario aroused by Riel's execution of Thomas Scott, a military expedition under Colonel G. J. Wolseley was ent to Fort Garry, arriving August 24, 1870.

The advance of settlement into the plains and later the north-west led to the negotiation of treaties in which the Indians agreed to surrender their general claims to the land in return for reserves and certain gifts and annuities. The bloodshed common along the American frontier was almost entirely avoided by means of this policy and as a result also of certain other factors, notably the tradition of law and order established by the Hudson's Bay Company and maintained by the North-west Mounted Police, and the existence in Canada of a considerable Métis population to serve as intermediaries between white and Indian.

OPENING THE WEST AND NORTH

A Gatling gun

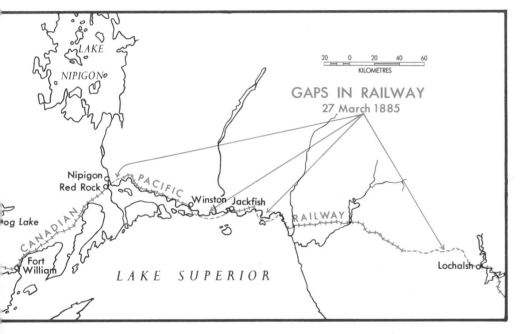

83　Gaps in the C.P.R.

For a variety of reasons, some resulting from errors or indifference on the part of the Government at Ottawa, the white settlers, part-Indians, and Indians of Canada's Northwest Territories were all becoming increasingly restless and discontented in the early 1880's. In 1884 at the invitation of his followers, Louis Riel returned from exile in the United States and on March 19, 1885, in spite of strong opposition from the Roman Catholic clergy, he proclaimed a provisional government at Batoche, the centre of Métis settlement in the Saskatchewan District. Not prepared to go to such an extreme, the settlers and people of part Indian, part English ancestry remained aloof as did the Indians of the great Blackfoot Confederacy and most of the Crees, except for bands led by Poundmaker and Big Bear. Nevertheless, when fighting began near Duck Lake on March 26, a mounted police and militia force was defeated and soon the whole area was in Métis or Indian hands except for weakly held positions at Prince Albert, Battleford, and Fort Saskatchewan.

Rapid suppression of the uprising before it could become widespread or well organized was made possible by the use of the telegraph to send immediate word to Ottawa and use of the Canadian Pacific Railway, completed except for a few gaps north of Lake Superior, to send troops (militia and some units of the new Permanent Force) to the scene. Two Gatling machine-guns and two small steamers on the South Saskatchewan were innovations to prairie warfare.

The advance against the rebels was made by three columns. The largest led by General Middleton moved cautiously north from Fort Qu'Appelle and after an indecisive encounter at Fish Creek (April 24), took Batoche (May 12) and captured Riel (May 15). Lieutenant-Colonel Otter pushed ahead rapidly from Swift Current and relieved civilians held for a month at the mercy of the Indians at Battleford (April 25), but was checked by Poundmaker in a skirmish at Cut Knife Hill (May 2). Major-General Strange reached Edmonton from Calgary and moved down the North Saskatchewan until stopped by Big Bear at Frenchman's Butte (May 28). Meanwhile Middleton had advanced to Battleford in mopping-up operations and accepted Poundmaker's surrender (May 26). He went on to join Strange near Fort Pitt and the rebellion ended when Big Bear gave himself up (July 2).

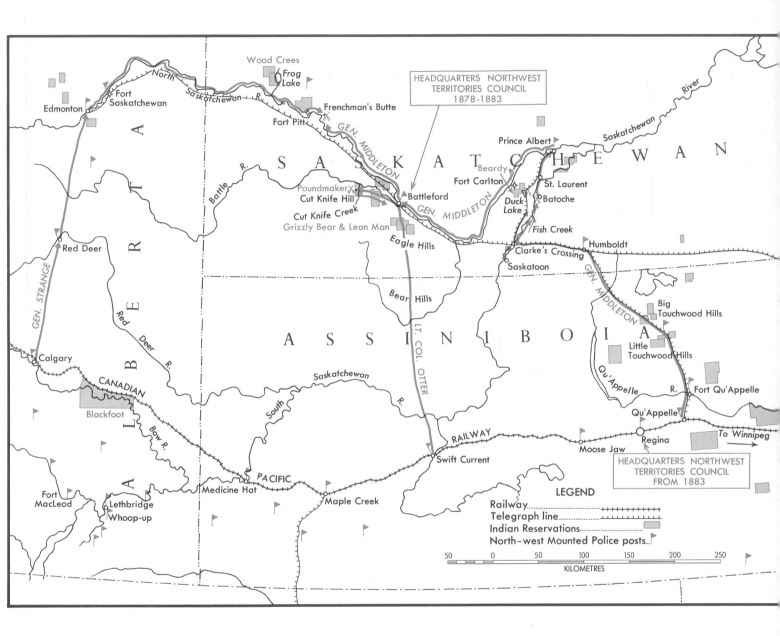

Wood Crees

Frog Lake

Edmonton

Fort Saskatchewan

North Saskatchewan R.

ALBERTA

Frenchman's Butte

Fort Pitt

GEN. MIDDLETON

HEADQUARTERS NORTHWEST TERRITORIES COUNCIL 1878-1883

River

Saskatchewan

SASKATCHEWAN

Prince Albert

Battle R.

Poundmaker X

Cut Knife Hill

Cut Knife Creek

Grizzly Bear & Lean Man

Eagle Hills

Battleford

GEN. MIDDLETON

Fort Carlton

Beardy

Duck Lake

St. Laurent

Batoche

Fish Creek

Clarke's Crossing

Saskatoon

Humboldt

GEN. MIDDLETON

GEN. STRANGE

Red Deer

Bear Hills

LT. COL. OTTER

ASSINIBOIA

Red Deer R.

Calgary

CANADIAN

Blackfoot

Bow R.

Saskatchewan

South

Saskatchewan R.

Big Touchwood Hills

Little Touchwood Hills

Qu'Appelle

Qu'Appelle R.

Fort Qu'Appelle

Qu'Appelle

RAILWAY

PACIFIC

Medicine Hat

Fort MacLeod

Lethbridge

Whoop-up

Maple Creek

Swift Current

Moose Jaw

Regina

To Winnipeg

HEADQUARTERS NORTHWEST TERRITORIES COUNCIL FROM 1883

LEGEND
Railway.............................
Telegraph line....................+++++++
Indian Reservations..............
North-west Mounted Police posts...

50   0   50   100   150   200   250
KILOMETRES

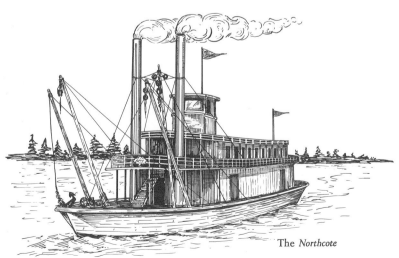

The *Northcote*

OPENING THE WEST AND NORTH

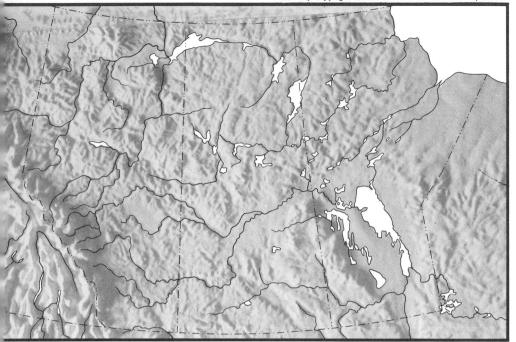

84 Relief

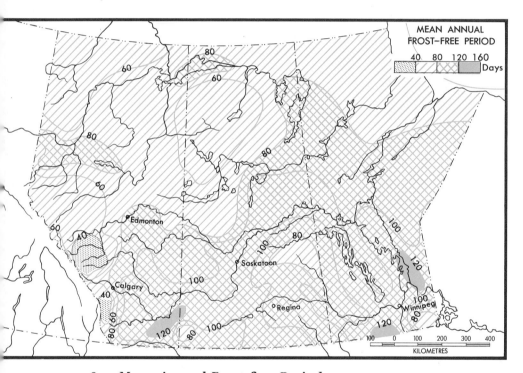

85 Mean Annual Frost-free Period

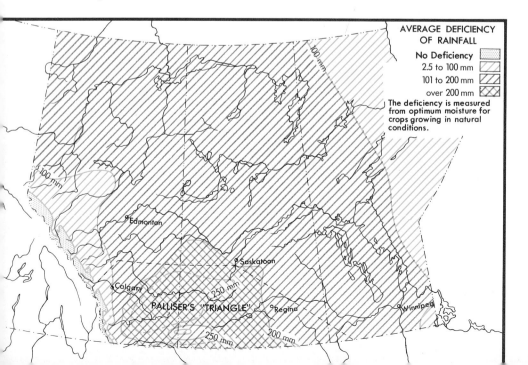

Physical Conditions in the Prairie Region

The suitability of the prairie region for agricultural settlement, long denied by Hudson's Bay Company officials, was investigated late in the 1850's by Captain John Palliser on behalf of the British Government and by S. J. Dawson and Professor H. Y. Hind for Canada. The findings of the Canadians at least, were quite optimistic with regard to a fertile belt between the south-western arid 'triangle', so called by Palliser, and the northern forests. As time went on factual knowledge of the region's physical features and their relationship to settlement was expanded by others, notably the somewhat over-enthusiastic John Macoun, a botanist who made his observations in the 1870's during preliminary surveys for the Canadian Pacific Railway.

Basic determinants of settlements have in fact been: (1) relief and topography; (2) the number of frost-free days normally to be expected between the last killing frost of spring and the first of fall; (3) aridity, a complex factor depending mainly on the amount of rainfall, especially during the growing season, but modified by other conditions such as excessive heat and evaporation; (4) the nature of the various soils, which in turn is partly dependent on the type of original vegetation—for example, the very rich dark-brown soils of the Park Belt are in the region distinguished by tall prairie grass and an annual rainfall of at least 380 mm.

Early adverse judgements of Hudson's Bay Company officials had not been simply the result of the fur trader's natural prejudice against settlement. They proved indeed to be sounder in many respects during the nineteenth century than Canadian optimism, the actual progress of settlement being very slow. It could be accelerated only after railway and other transportation facilities had been laboriously provided, dry farming and improved agricultural machinery had been developed, and quick-maturing strains of wheat had been introduced—Red Fife by 1900, Marquis by 1912, and Garnet and Reward by 1929.

86 Average Deficiency of Rainfall

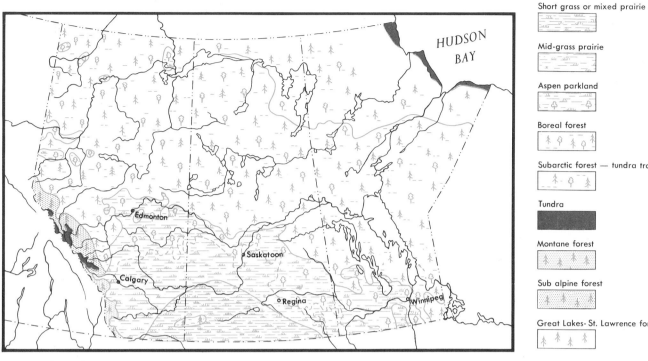

87 Vegetation

LEGEND

Short grass or mixed prairie

Mid-grass prairie

Aspen parkland

Boreal forest

Subarctic forest — tundra transition

Tundra

Montane forest

Sub alpine forest

Great Lakes- St. Lawrence forest

88 Soil Types

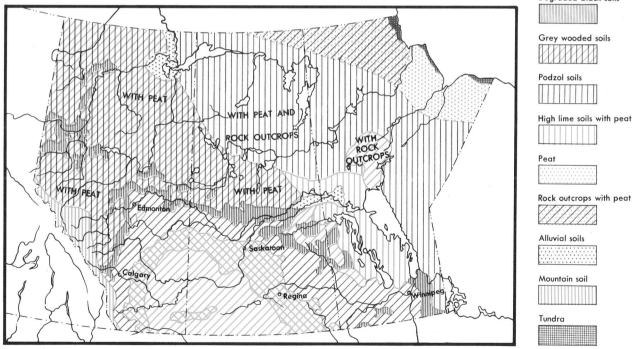

Brown soils

Dark brown soils

Black soils

Degraded black soils

Grey wooded soils

Podzol soils

High lime soils with peat

Peat

Rock outcrops with peat

Alluvial soils

Mountain soil

Tundra

OPENING THE WEST AND NORTH

The Disposal of Prairie Lands

The transfer of Rupert's Land and the Northwest Territories to Canada (July 15, 1870) vested in the federal government ownership of a vast public domain five times the previous area of the whole Dominion. By terms of the transfer the Hudson's Bay Company retained blocks around the trading posts not exceeding a total of 20 234 ha and also one-twentieth of the land in a fertile belt defined as bounded by the United States, the Rocky Mountains, the North Saskatchewan, and Lake Winnipeg, Lake of the Woods and the waters linking them. The Company's twentieth eventually amounted to 2 686 694 ha. A small quantity of land

had already passed into private hands during the Hudson's Bay régime, more was set aside from time to time for Indian reserves, and generous grants were made to people of part Indian descent, to settlers of the Selkirk period, to members of Wolseley's expedition, and to others. There remained nevertheless enormous 'dominion lands' used by the federal government for the next sixty years for the interlocking purposes of promoting settlement and railway building. Major events in this connection occurred as follows: (1) April 25, 1871. An order in council initiated a great and almost completely uniform land survey in which each township

was six miles (9.7 km) square and contained 36 sections, each section containing 640 acres (259 ha) and being a square mile (2.6 km²) in both size and shape. Townships were numbered northward from a base line on the American border, ranges of townships east and west from a principal meridian running through Fort Garry and then, farther westward, from five other principal meridians. Sections were numbered from the south-east corner of each township. Only minor modifications were later made in this general pattern, for example, in connection with the river lots of the part-Indian people on the Red, South Saskatchewan, Bow, Belly, and Red Deer rivers and

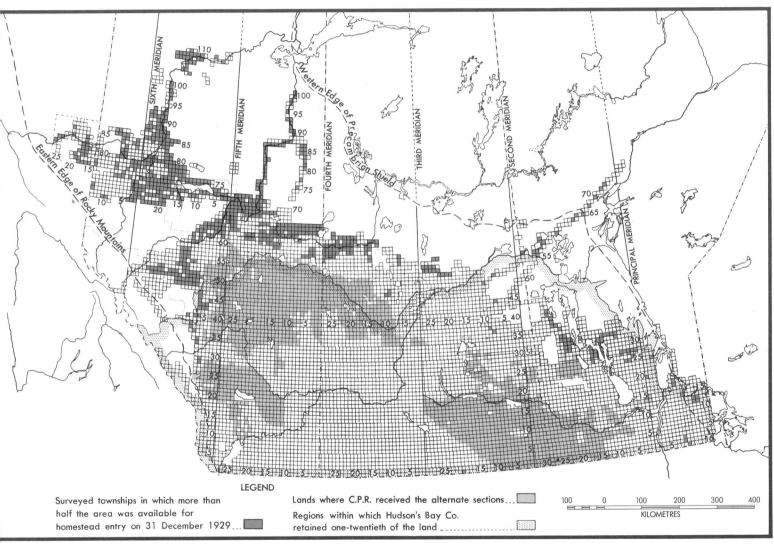

LEGEND

Surveyed townships in which more than half the area was available for homestead entry on 31 December 1929...

Lands where C.P.R. received the alternate sections...

Regions within which Hudson's Bay Co. retained one-twentieth of the land

100 0 100 200 300 400
KILOMETRES

89   The Prairie Land Survey

90   A Prairie Township

LEGEND

Free homestead lands....

School lands............

Railway lands...........

Hudson's Bay Co. lands...

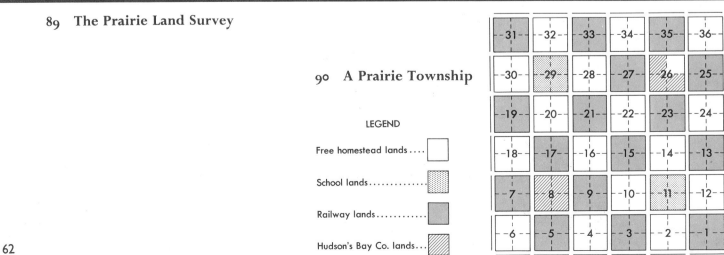

the irrigation lands of the Canadian Pacific Railway.

(2) April 14, 1872. The first Dominion Lands Act laid down basic policies including provision for free quarter-section homestead grants, reservation of sections 11 and 29 in each township to endow public schools, and allocation of section 8 and three-quarters of section 26 (the whole of 26 in every fifth township) to meet Hudson's Bay Company claims.

(3) October 21, 1880. The contract with the Canadian Pacific Railway syndicate provided, among other things, for a grant of 10 117 000 ha 'fairly fit for settlement' in the region between Winnipeg and the Rockies. In a belt 39 km on either side of its main line the railway would have the right to alternate sections (odd-numbered sections) except for any rejected as unfit and it could make up the rest by choosing odd-numbered sections elsewhere. Modifications of these arrangements were made later, but in all, on account of main- and branch-line grants and others made to subsidiaries, the Canadian Pacific Railway eventually acquired a total of 10 544 124 ha. Grants to other 'colonization' railways totalled another 2 318 044 ha and became based on the amount that the railway could 'earn', that is, 2590 ha in odd-numbered sections for every 1.6 km built.

(4) July 20, 1908. The new Dominion Lands Act included provision for liquidating the railway land-grant system. This system had served its purpose. The remaining odd-numbered sections were to be released for sale by the government. However, the revenue so obtained would be used to build the Hudson Bay Railway as a public enterprise. By 1929 when that line was completed receipts amounted to $21 992 174.

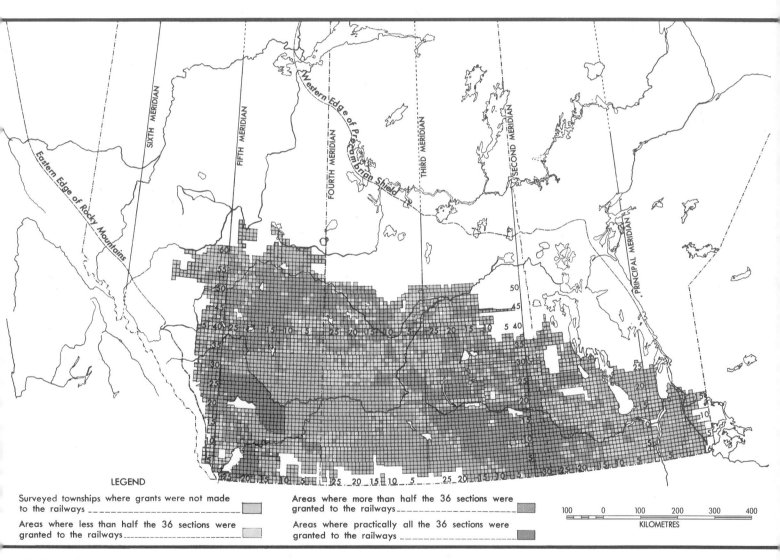

LEGEND

Surveyed townships where grants were not made to the railways _____

Areas where less than half the 36 sections were granted to the railways _____

Areas where more than half the 36 sections were granted to the railways _____

Areas where practically all the 36 sections were granted to the railways _____

100   0   100   200   300   400
KILOMETRES

91   Railway Land Grants to January 1, 1909

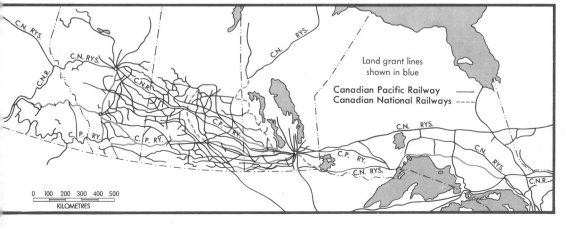

92
Railways
Built under the
Land Grant System

Land grant lines shown in blue

Canadian Pacific Railway ——
Canadian National Railways ----

0 100 200 300 400 500
KILOMETRES

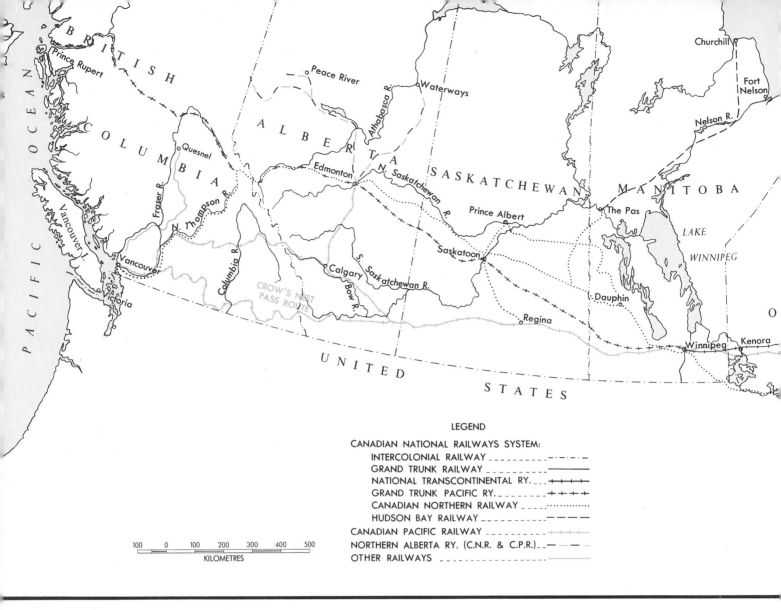

100 0 100 200 300 400 500
KILOMETRES

The Transportation Problem

Land grants and other aid from all levels of government were largely responsible for the rapid progress in railway building after Confederation. Total length in 1867 was 3666 km; in 1900, 28 415 km; in 1914, 49 588 km; and in 1931, 68 041 km. The main line of the first transcontinental, the Canadian Pacific Railway, was completed in November, 1885. Encouraged by the flood-tide of migration to the West in the 1890's and 1900's, a railway boom took place which covered the prairies with a network of feeder lines and resulted in the emergence of two more transcontinental systems. The first, the Grand Trunk Pacific between Prince Rupert and Winnipeg, a subsidiary of the Grand Trunk, was intended to be operated in conjunction with the National Transcontinental built by the federal government from Winnipeg to Moncton, N.B. The second, the Canadian Northern from Vancouver to Montreal, was built and pieced together by William Mackenzie and Donald Mann. Both lines were in serious difficulty by 1917 due partly to over-building and partly to the outbreak of the First World War which occurred as they were being completed and delayed further immigration and western development. Accordingly, in the period 1917–23 it became necessary for the federal government to take over the Canadian Northern, the Grand Trunk Pacific, and the Grand Trunk and consolidate them along with the government-built National Transcontinental, Intercolonial, and Prince Edward Island Railways to form the Canadian National Railways system. The Hudson Bay Railway, completed in 1929, was later added to this. The Canadian Pacific Railway and som smaller companies remained independent.

Meanwhile, to handle the large volume c grain beginning to flow from the prairie improvements had to be made as well in th vital St. Lawrence-Great Lakes waterwa stretching inland 3569 km from the Stra of Belle Isle to Port Arthur and Fo William. This involved enlarging or repla ing canals built before 1850. Beginning the 1870's, but mainly around the turn of th century, all were deepened from 2.7 m t at least 4.3 m. In addition, the ocea shipping channel down river from Montre was dredged to a depth of 9.1 (later 10. metres and extensive elevator and oth harbour facilities were provided at a numb of ports.

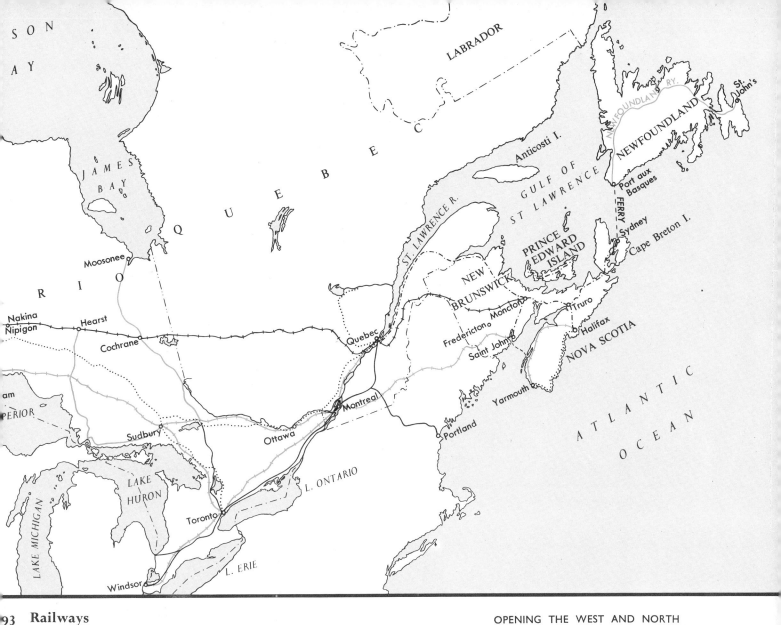

94 Canal Improvements

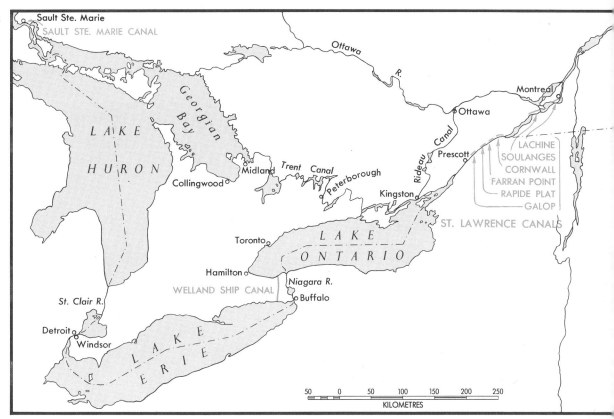

Sault Ste. Marie
SAULT STE. MARIE CANAL

Ottawa R.

Montreal

Ottawa

LAKE HURON

Georgian Bay

Rideau Canal

Prescott

LACHINE
SOULANGES
CORNWALL
FARRAN POINT
RAPIDE PLAT
GALOP

ST. LAWRENCE CANALS

Midland

Trent Canal

Peterborough

Collingwood

Kingston

Toronto

LAKE ONTARIO

Hamilton

WELLAND SHIP CANAL

Niagara R.

St. Clair R.

Buffalo

LAKE ERIE

Detroit
Windsor

50 0 50 100 150 200 250
KILOMETRES

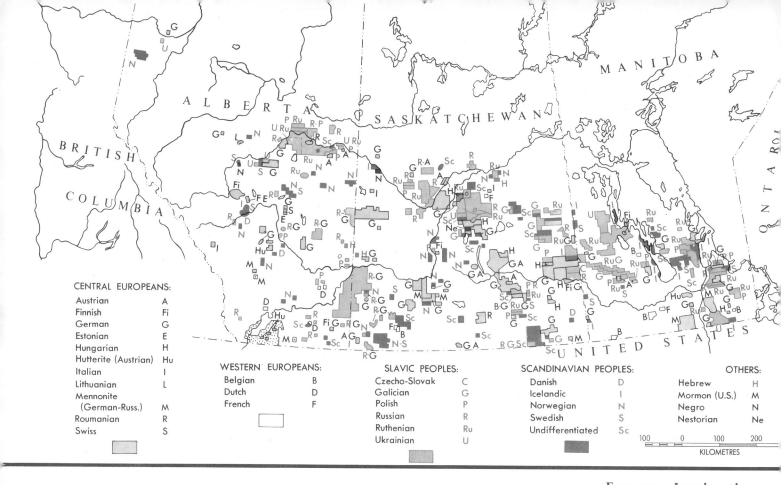

CENTRAL EUROPEANS:

Austrian	A
Finnish	Fi
German	G
Estonian	E
Hungarian	H
Hutterite (Austrian)	Hu
Italian	I
Lithuanian	L
Mennonite (German-Russ.)	M
Roumanian	R
Swiss	S

WESTERN EUROPEANS:

Belgian	B
Dutch	D
French	F

SLAVIC PEOPLES:

Czecho-Slovak	C
Galician	G
Polish	P
Russian	R
Ruthenian	Ru
Ukrainian	U

SCANDINAVIAN PEOPLES:

Danish	D
Icelandic	I
Norwegian	N
Swedish	S
Undifferentiated	Sc

OTHERS:

Hebrew	H
Mormon (U.S.)	M
Negro	N
Nestorian	Ne

100 0 100 200
KILOMETRES

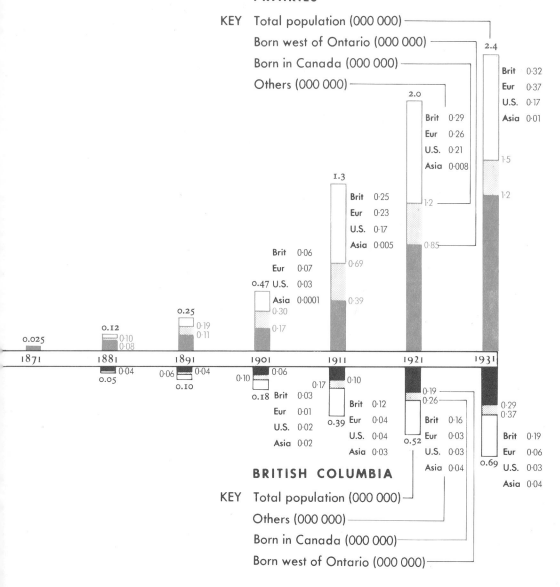

PRAIRIES

KEY Total population (000 000)
Born west of Ontario (000 000)
Born in Canada (000 000)
Others (000 000)

2.4
Brit 0·32
Eur 0·37
U.S. 0·17
Asia 0·01
1·5
1·2

2.0
Brit 0·29
Eur 0·26
U.S. 0·21
Asia 0·008
1·2
0·85

1.3
Brit 0·25
Eur 0·23
U.S. 0·17
Asia 0·005
0·69
0·39

Brit 0·06
Eur 0·07
0.47 U.S. 0·03
Asia 0·0001
0·30
0·17

0.25
0·19
0·11

0.12
0·10
0·08

0.025

| 1871 | 1881 | 1891 | 1901 | 1911 | 1921 | 1931 |

0·05
0·04

0·06 0·04
0·10

0·10 0·06
0·18 Brit 0·03
Eur 0·01
U.S. 0·02
Asia 0·02

0·17 0·10
0·39 Brit 0·12
Eur 0·04
U.S. 0·04
Asia 0·03

0·19
0·26
0·52 Brit 0·16
Eur 0·03
U.S. 0·03
Asia 0·04

0·29
0·37
0·69 Brit 0·19
Eur 0·06
U.S. 0·03
Asia 0·04

BRITISH COLUMBIA

KEY Total population (000 000)
Others (000 000)
Born in Canada (000 000)
Born west of Ontario (000 000)

---

96 The Growth and Origins of Population

Gradual completion of railways, incr[easing] scarcity of new land in the United S[tates] and the encouragement afforded immig[ration] by agencies of the government and th[e rail-] way companies were major factors ca[using] an accelerated growth of population i[n the] Canadian West in the late nineteent[h and] early twentieth centuries. A high prop[ortion] of the immigrants were from v[arious] European countries and many settl[ed in] separate national groups. Differing [from] the majority in language, traditions, an[d fre-] quently in religion, these 'New Cana[dians'] tended to be slow in assimilation and t[o give] the prairie population a distinctive char[acter.] In British Columbia, Asiatic immigrat[ion as] well was significant.

The Administration of the Wes[t] and North

Following the transfer of Rupert's Lan[d and] the Northwest Territories to C[anada] (July 15, 1870), the province of Man[itoba] was created as provided for in the Man[itoba] Act (May 12, 1870) and the administ[ration] of the remaining unorganized Nort[hwest]

Territories was undertaken by a lieutenant-governor appointed by the federal government. Part of this region became the separate District of Keewatin in 1876. A further transfer from Britain to Canada of the Arctic Islands took place on September 1, 1880.

On July 1, 1881, the boundaries of Manitoba were enlarged somewhat and on the east they became common with the western border of Ontario. This led to a renewal of Ontario's long-standing claim to western and northern territories far beyond the limits the Canadian government was willing to acknowledge—a claim based on earlier disputes going back to French Canada and the Hudson's Bay Company and to the Quebec Act and Guy Carleton's commission as governor (see Map 42). The question had been submitted to arbitrators in 1878 but their award had not been accepted by the federal government. In 1884, it was taken before the Judicial Committee of the Privy Council which upheld the 1878 award. Eventually, in 1889, the Committee's decision was embodied in an Imperial act adding considerably to the previously recognized area of Ontario. A Canadian act of 1898 made a corresponding addition to the size of Quebec extending its boundary northward to the Eastmain River. Meanwhile, in 1882 a Canadian order in council had created the provisional districts of Assiniboia, Saskatchewan, Athabaska, and Alberta and provided for their government by a lieutenant-governor with his capital at Regina in Saskatchewan. A further order in council in 1895 created similar districts of Ungava, Franklin, Mackenzie, and Yukon, while one in 1897 made alterations in their boundaries and in those of the District of Keewatin as well. Following the discovery of gold on the Klondike (August, 1896), the District of Yukon was more fully organized as the separate Yukon Territory on June 13, 1898.

By 1905, growth of population in the prairie region was such that two new provinces, Saskatchewan and Alberta, were created. The District of Keewatin, governed to that time by the lieutenant-governor of Manitoba, was incorporated into the Northwest Territories. In 1912, the boundaries of Manitoba, Ontario, and Quebec were enlarged to their present limits.

Further changes in the boundaries of the Mackenzie, Keewatin, and Franklin Districts came into effect in 1920, the Quebec-Labrador boundary was defined by the Judicial Committee of the Privy Council in 1927, and by 1931 Canada's territorial claims extended to the North Pole.

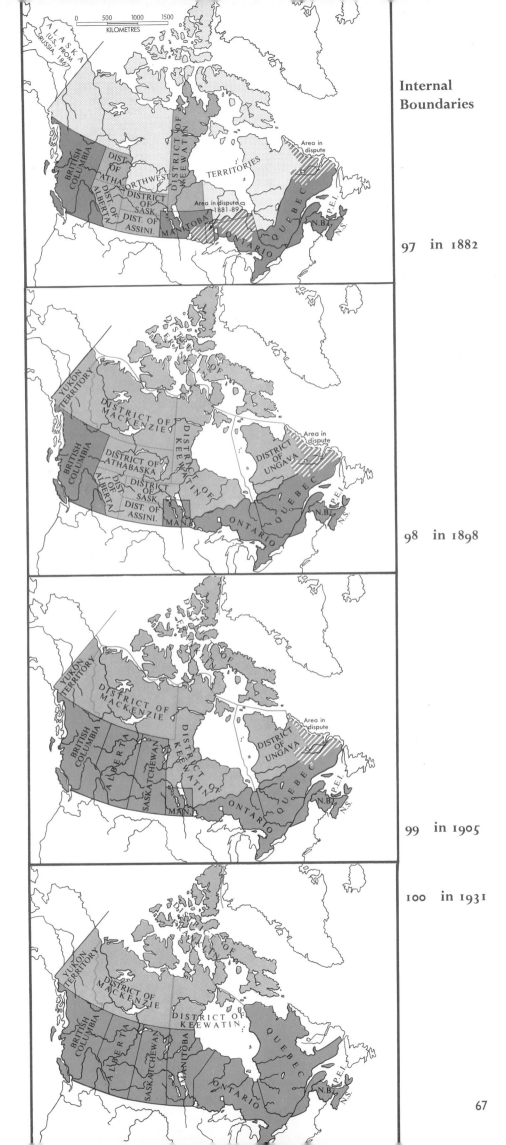

Internal Boundaries

97 in 1882

98 in 1898

99 in 1905

100 in 1931

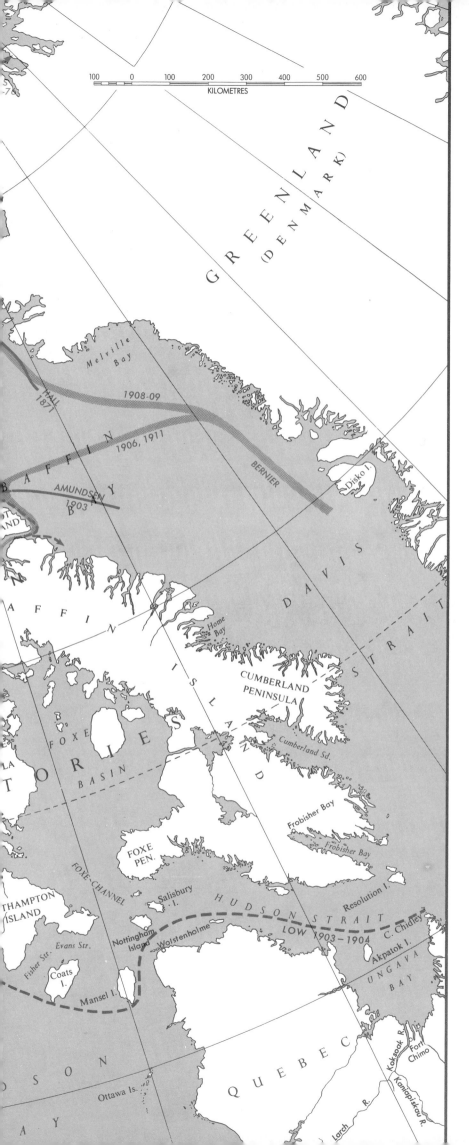

101 Northern Discovery and Scientific Exploration

Commercial and scientific, political and personal motives led to a renewal of interest in the Arctic beginning in the last quarter of the nineteenth century. Whaling fleets operating in Baffin Bay on the east and the Beaufort Sea on the west became increasingly familiar with adjacent coasts and inlets, while the Hudson's Bay Company, followed shortly by a few private traders, began opening Arctic trading posts, the first at Wolstenholme in 1909. British, American, Norwegian, Canadian, and other expeditions —only a few of which can be shown on a single map—added gradually to knowledge of the region. Many leaders, including the British Admiralty's Nares (1875), hoped to be the first to reach the North Pole. This was finally done by Peary of the American Navy (1909). Norway's Amundsen realized (1903–6), at the cost of three Arctic winters, the other old dream of navigating a Northwest Passage.

From the days of Henry Hudson, however, initial discoveries had been British (Sverdrup's Norwegian expedition, 1898–1902, would constitute the sole major exception) and Britain's claim to sovereignty in the North American Arctic west of Greenland had therefore long been recognized. After September 1, 1880, when Britain transferred her rights to Canada, the latter's interest became paramount. Canadian Government expeditions under such men as Tyrrell, Low, Bernier, and Stefansson then began collecting the detailed navigational and scientific information on which future Arctic advances could be based.

OPENING THE WEST AND NORTH

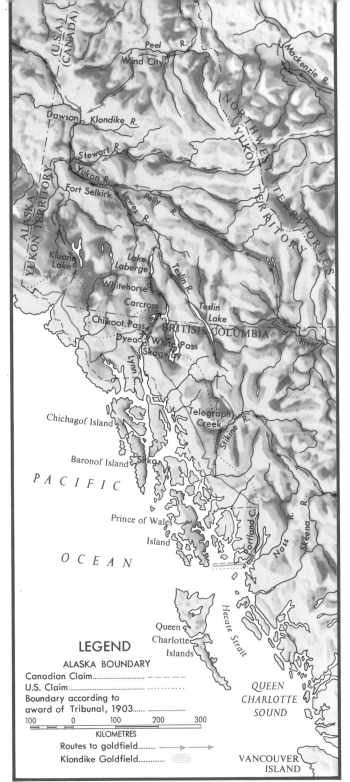

Base map copyright Canadian Aero Service Limited, Ottawa

LEGEND

ALASKA BOUNDARY

Canadian Claim.................. – – –
U.S. Claim........................... ············
Boundary according to
award of Tribunal, 1903......– ——

100   0   100   200   300

KILOMETRES

Routes to goldfield........... ——→
Klondike Goldfield..............

102 Klondike Gold and the Alaska Boundary

The last great gold rush followed reports in August, 1896, of discoveries in Bonanza Creek, a tributary of the Klondike near Dawson City. In the next few years miners poured in, mainly by ship up the Lynn Canal to Dyea or Skagway and thence through the Chilkoot and White Passes and down 800 km of the Lewes and Yukon Rivers to Dawson. Others made their way up the Stikine River or even by way of the Mackenzie and Porcupine. Dawson rapidly acquired a population of 25 000 and annual gold production rose to a maximum, in 1900, of over 35 000 000 g.

Rival claims of Canada and the United States to the ports at the head of the Lynn Canal, based on differing interpretations of the Anglo-Russian Treaty of 1825 (see Map 57), became of immediate importance. They were finally settled in favour of the United States by a joint Anglo-American tribunal appointed in 1903 to define the whole Canada-Alaska boundary. Two of the three British arbitrators were Canadians who dissented from the majority decision.

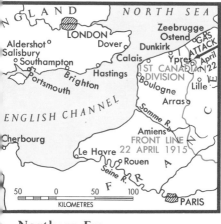

Northern France

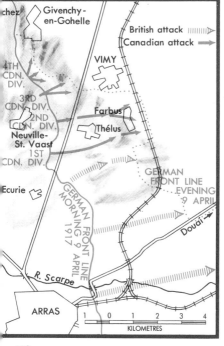

Vimy, 1917

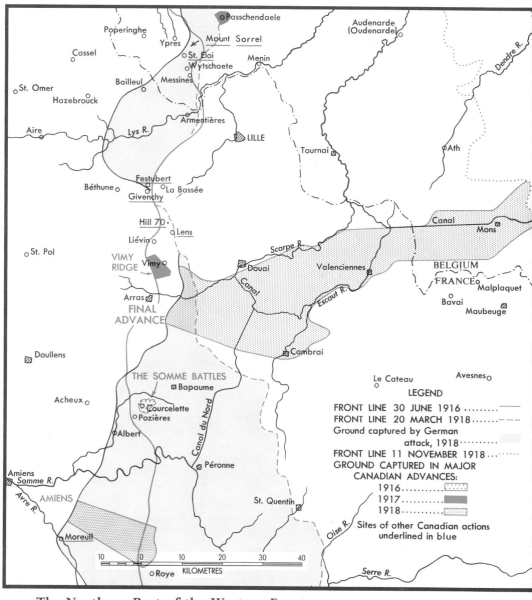

105   The Northern Part of the Western Front

The First World War

Canada entered the First World War automatically when Britain did on August 4, 1914, and the First Canadian Contingent, 33 000 strong, embarked for overseas service two months later (October 3). Others followed and a Canadian Corps was eventually formed under the successive commands of Lieutenant-General E. A. H. Alderson, Lieutenant-General Sir Julian Byng, and finally the first Canadian, Lieutenant-General Sir Arthur Currie (June 23, 1917).

1915. The Canadians' battle experience began with the famous defensive struggle commonly called the Second Battle of Ypres (April 22–7) when they held their line in spite of the Germans' first use of poison gas. Fighting at Festubert and Givenchy (May 20–6) followed with heavy losses.

1916. The Canadians took part in engagements at St. Eloi (April 3–20) and Mount Sorrel (June 1–3) before being transferred in August from Flanders to the Somme to assist in the great and futile allied offensive there, their only real success being the capture of Courcelette (September 15).

1917. The taking of Vimy Ridge (April 9), the first occasion when all four Canadian divisions attacked together, was followed by victory at Hill 70 (August 15) and the bloody battle for Passchendaele (October 26–November 10).

1918. After a major success at Amiens (August 8) the Canadians broke through the Drocourt-Quéant line (September 2–4), took Cambrai (October 1–9), and were in Mons when the Armistice came (November 11).

106   Axis Domination of Europe, 1942

107   The Battle of the Atlantic

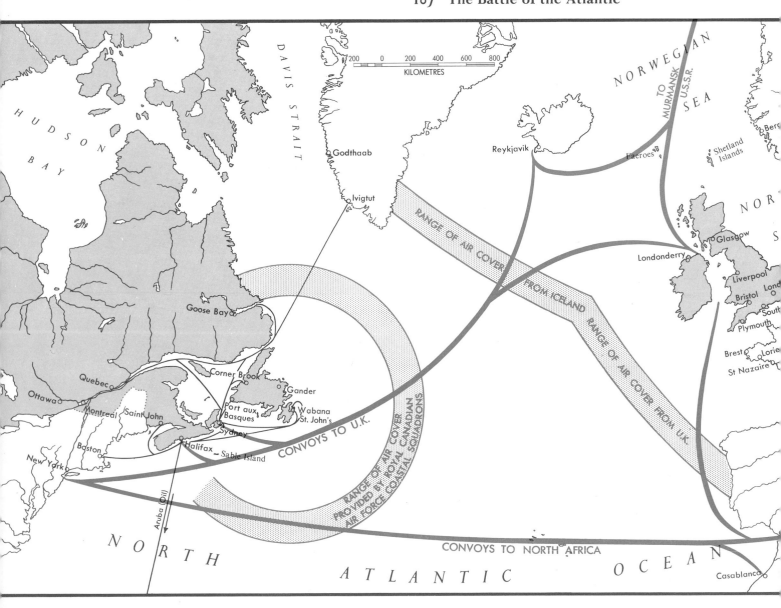

The Second World War

Germany's invasion of Poland on September 1, 1939, led to declarations of war by Britain and France (September 3) and various other allied powers including Canada (September 10). Already in occupation of Austria and Czechoslovakia, the Germans swept rapidly through Poland, entered Denmark and Norway (April 9, 1940), defeated the Low Countries and France, which signed an Armistice (June 22, 1940), and invaded Russia (June 21, 1941). Meanwhile they had been joined by the Italians (June 10, 1940) and when on December 7, 1941, the Japanese struck at the American base of Pearl Harbour and British and Dutch possessions in the Far East the conflict became world-wide. By mid-1942, almost the whole of Europe and North Africa was under the domination of the Rome-Berlin Axis while much of the Pacific, south-east Asia, and China were controlled by Japan.

A major contribution of the Canadian navy throughout the war was helping to protect, with her corvettes, frigates, and other escort vessels, the life-stream of supplies and reinforcements flowing from North America to Britain across the cold, stormy, and U-boat-infested North Atlantic. The air force shared in this task, in the great Commonwealth Air Training Plan based in Canada, and in allied fighting, bombing, and reconnaissance generally.

The army's first major opportunity came with the invasion of Sicily. Canadian forces joined the British and Americans, fresh from victories in North Africa, to help capture that island (July–August, 1943) and cross to the mainland of Italy (September 3). In heavy street fighting during the Christmas season they drove the Germans out of Ortona (December 21–8). The next spring, the First Canadian Corps broke the Adolf Hitler Line across the Liri valley (May 23). In the autumn, back on the Adriatic Coast, it breached the Gothic Line along the Foglia River (August 30–September 3) and entered the broad Po Valley where the line was stabilized for the winter. The First Corps moved to north-west Europe early in 1945.

108 The Italian Campaign

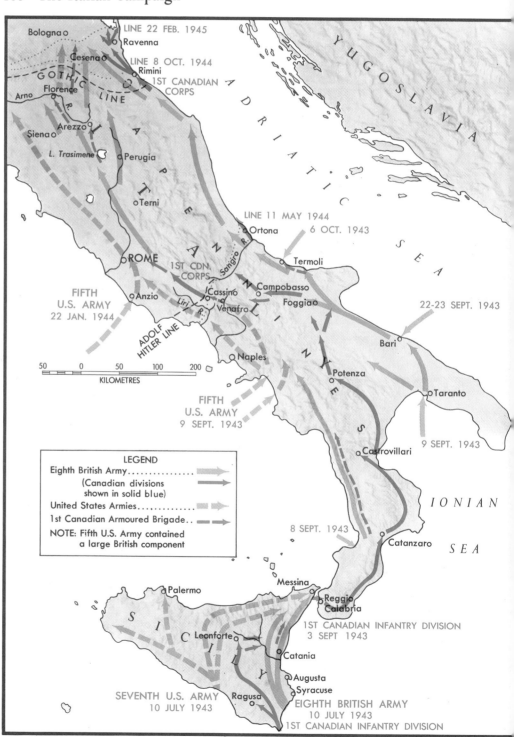

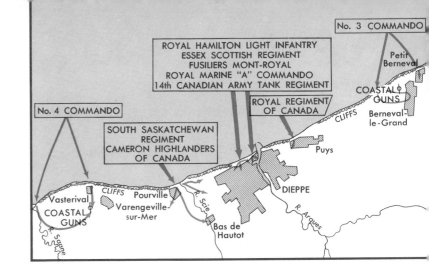

109 The Dieppe Raid

110 Invasion and Victory

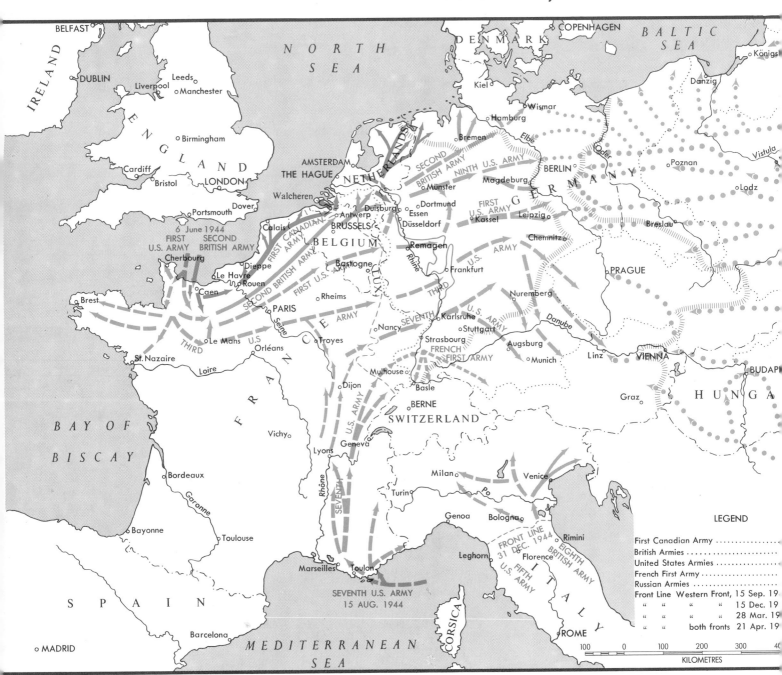

A landing craft

The Dieppe Raid (August 19, 1942), undertaken by Canadians, supported by British commando units to which some American and Free French soldiers were attached, tried the strength of Hitler's continental defences. It cost Canada 3350 casualties out of some 5000 participants.

This lesson was not forgotten in the elaborate planning that preceded the final allied landings in Normandy (June 6, 1944). One Canadian division took part in these and in the strategically important capture of Caen (July 9). Soon afterwards the First Canadian Army became operational (July 23) and by hard persistent fighting took Falaise (August 17) helping, along with the Americans at Argentan, to close the gap through which the Germans had hoped to escape from their lost battlefields of Normandy.

Turning north-eastward along the allied left flank, the Canadians went on to clear the Channel ports (including Dieppe), eliminate flying-bomb sites, and finally wear down German resistance in South Beveland and Walcheren, opening the Scheldt and its vital port of Antwerp by November 28.

Remaining on the flank when the last great allied offensive began in February, 1945, they battered stubbornly through the defences of the Reichswald and Hochwald region until, with the allied crossing of the Rhine in several sectors, German strength began to crumble. Mopping-up operations in the northern Netherlands and adjacent parts of Germany concluded with the German surrender on May 7.

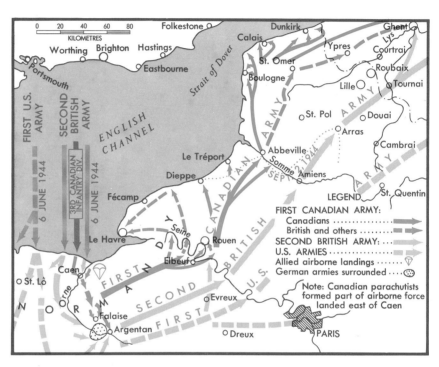

111   **From Normandy to the Channel Ports**

112   **The Netherlands and German Campaigns**

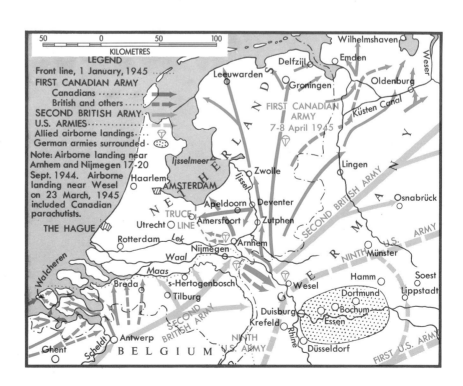

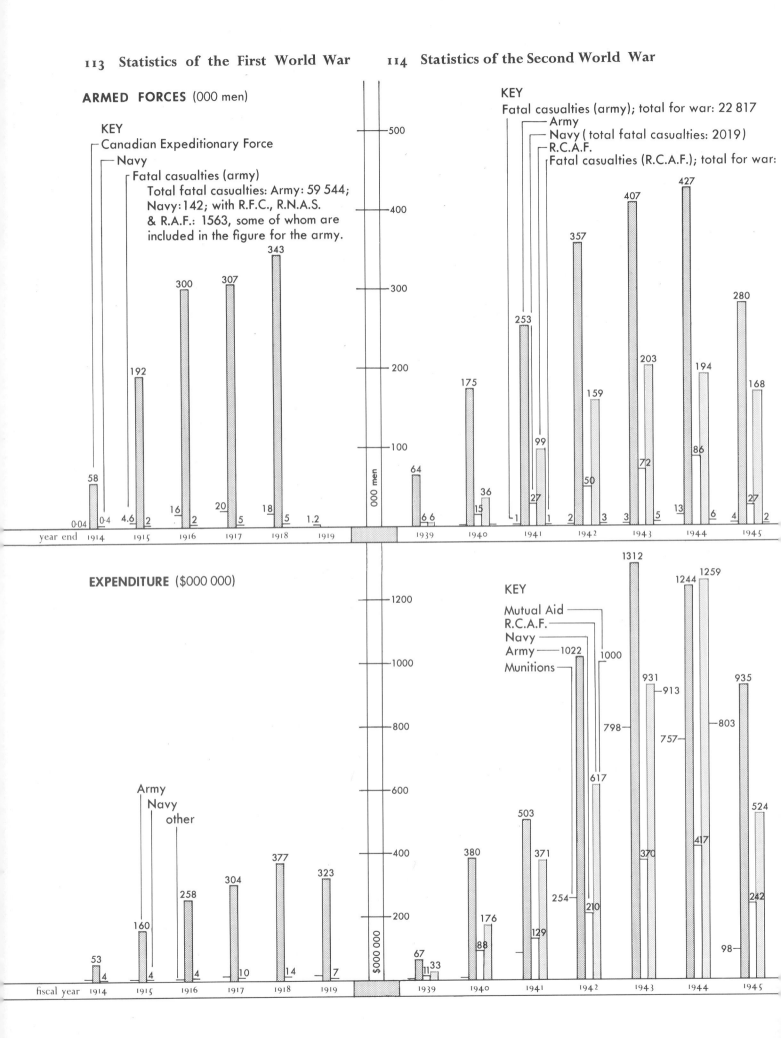

113 Statistics of the First World War · **114 Statistics of the Second World War**

ARMED FORCES (000 men)

KEY
- Canadian Expeditionary Force
- Navy
- Fatal casualties (army)
  Total fatal casualties: Army: 59 544;
  Navy: 142; with R.F.C., R.N.A.S.
  & R.A.F.: 1563, some of whom are
  included in the figure for the army.

KEY
Fatal casualties (army); total for war: 22 817
- Army
- Navy (total fatal casualties: 2019)
- R.C.A.F.
- Fatal casualties (R.C.A.F.); total for war:

000 men

year end | 1914 | 1915 | 1916 | 1917 | 1918 | 1919 | 1939 | 1940 | 1941 | 1942 | 1943 | 1944 | 1945

EXPENDITURE ($000 000)

Army
Navy
other

KEY
- Mutual Aid
- R.C.A.F.
- Navy
- Army — 1022
- Munitions

$000 000

fiscal year | 1914 | 1915 | 1916 | 1917 | 1918 | 1919 | 1939 | 1940 | 1941 | 1942 | 1943 | 1944 | 1945

Newfoundland's union with Canada was proposed at the time of the original Confederation discussions in the 1860's, again after a disastrous bank failure in 1894, and once more during the First World War. All change was resisted however until 1934 when, as a result of financial collapse brought on by the depression, the eighty-year-old system of Responsible Government had to be abandoned and Newfoundland reverted to colonial status under a Commission of Government appointed by Britain. During the Second World War the establishment of Canadian and American air and naval bases brought unprecedented prosperity. Afterwards the question arose: Should Newfoundland's independence be restored or should she join Canada or possibly the United States? The answer was given when on March 31, 1949, Newfoundland became Canada's tenth province.

The island's economy, dependent from the earliest days on the fisheries, had always lacked stability. The remedy of diversification was difficult to achieve. Soil and climate forbade all but the most modest amount of agriculture. Iron mining, which began on Bell Island in 1895, and the building of the Corner Brook paper mill in 1925 were the two most hopeful signs of progress. The meandering trans-island railway, completed from St. John's to Port aux Basques in 1897, helped open the interior but remained a constant financial burden. In 1923, it had to be taken over by the government, along with essential steamship and telegraph services. Second World War prosperity, however, and Confederation seemed likely to produce an upward trend, especially since the Confederation Agreement included provision for quite large federal subsidies, federal maintenance of certain transportation facilities, and federal acceptance of responsibility for the existing provincial debt. Recent developments include the extensive iron-mining operations in the Labrador trough and the enormous hydro-power installations at Churchill Falls, while modernization is changing the structure of the fishing industry and there is fuller utilization of mineral and forest resources.

115 Confederation with Newfoundland

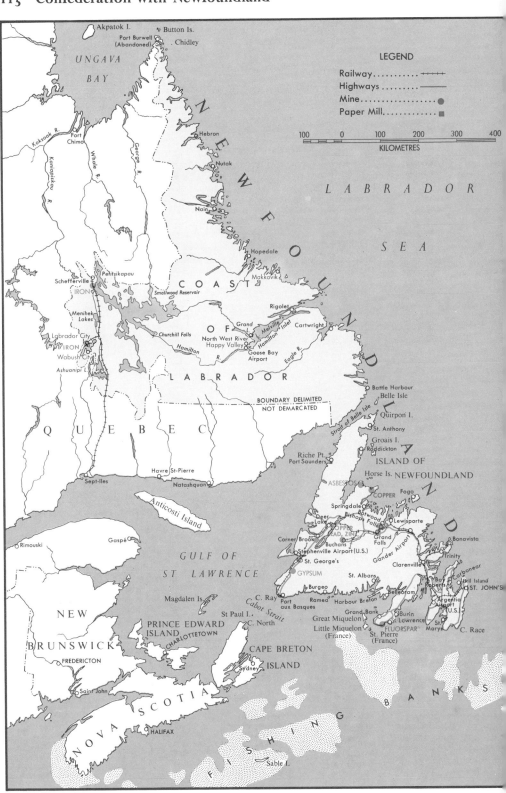

U.S. submarine "Nautilus" from Point Barrow, 1 August 1958 under ice to North Pole (3 August) and on to Atlantic Ocean between Spitsbergen and Greenland (5 August).

ARCTIC   OCEAN

QUEEN   ELIZABETH

ISLANDS

BEAUFORT

SEA

APPROXIMATE LIMIT OF PERMANENT POLAR ICE

"MANHATTAN" 1969

Prudhoe Bay

Herschel

U.S.A.
CANADA

Mackenzie
Bay Tuktoyaktuk
Old Crow
Aklavik
Fort
McPherson
Arctic Red
River
Inuvik
Reindeer Station

Sachs Harbour

BANKS

ISLAND

Prince of Wales Str.

ST-ROCH
1940-41-41
AMUNDSEN GULF
Cape
Parry
1944

Anderson R.

Prince Albert Sd.

WOLLASTON
PEN.

Horton R.

Holman I.

Dolphin and Union Str.

Read I.

DISTRICT

VICTORIA

ISLAND

MELVILLE   ISLAND

PARRY   ISLANDS

PRINCE
PATRICK I.

Mould
Bay

M'Clure Str.

VISCOUNT   MELVILLE SOUND

Stefansson
I.

M'CLINTOCK CHAN.

PRINCE

OF

WALES

ISLAND

Borden I.

Mackenzie
King
I.

HAZEN STRAIT

Prince Gustaf Adolf Sea

Isachsen

Cornwall I.

Belcher Chan.

Ellef
Ringnes

Amund
Ringnes
I.

SVERDRUP   ISLANDS

AXEL
HEIBERG
ISLAND

Meighen I.

Norwegian
Bay

Eureka

Grise Fi.

Jones Sound

DEVON IS

BATHURST I.

Wellington Chan.

Cornwallis I.
Resolute

Barrow Str.

PARRY   CHANNEL   LANCAS

ST-ROCH

Peel Sd.

SOMERSET
ISLAND

Prince Regent In.

Bellot Str.

GULF

OF

BOOTHIA

BOOTH

WINTER
1941-42

James Ross Str.

BOOTHIA
PEN.

BRODEUR PEN.

FR

Coppermine

Coronation Gulf

Dease Str.

Cambridge
Bay

Victoria Str.

KING
WILLIAM
I. Gjoa
Haven

Queen Maud Gulf

"ST-ROCH"

Perry Island

Pelly Bay

Pelly Bay

Chantrey In.

Spence
Bay

NORTH   WEST   TER

Coppermine R.

Hood R.

Bathurst Inlet

ARCTIC CIRCLE

DISTRICT

OF

Fort Franklin
Great Bear
R.
Fort Norman

Great Bear
Lake

Port Radium

Sawmill Bay

Camsell R.

Contwoyto L.

Point L.

Garry L. Macdougall

Pelly L.

Schultz L.
Baker
Lake

DISTRICT

OF

KEEWATIN

Chesterfield I

Chesterfield Inlet

YUKON

TERRITORY

Peel R.

Fort Good Hope

MACKENZIE

Norman Wells

Wrigley

Lac La
Martre

Rae

Discovery

Aylmer L.
Clinton
Colden
Lake

Artillery L.

Fort Reliance

Thelon R.

Wharton L.

Dubawnt L.

Baker L.

M A C K E N Z I E

Watson
Lake

ALASKA

Liard River

Fort Nelson

South
Nahanni R.

Nahanni Butte

Fort
Simpson

Livingston's Fort

Fort Liard

RIVER

Hay River

MACKENZIE HWY.

Fort
Providence

Great Slave
Lake

Rocher
River

Yellowknife

Snowdrift

Taltson R.

Fort Resolution

Fort Smith

Great Slave R.

Hay
River

BRITISH   COLUMBIA

ALBERTA

Wholdaia L.

Selwyn L.

Kasba L.

Dubawnt R.

Kazan R.

Nueltin Lake

Thlewiaza R.

Tha-anne R.

Eskimo Point

116 Exploration and Mapping

Defence requirements and scientific advances opened a new era of Arctic exploration during and especially after the Second World War. The spectacular individual achievements characteristic of earlier periods were rare – although they included the famous voyages eastward (1940–2) and westward (1944) through a North-west Passage by the R.C.M.P. schooner *St. Roch*, and that eastward, for the first time beneath the Arctic ice, of the United States Navy's atomic submarine *Nautilus* (1958). In 1969 the oil tanker *Manhattan* became the first commercial vessel to make its way through the North-west Passage, testing the feasibility of a shipping route through the Canadian Arctic from the oil fields of the Alaska North Slope.

The real achievement of this period, however, was the steady accumulation of detailed and exact knowledge by government, university, and commercial expeditions year after year. Modern devices and equipment, especially radio and the aeroplane, allowed hitherto impossible feats to be accomplished. After R. E. Byrd's flight over the North Pole in 1926, the aeroplane rapidly became the means of opening new posts and settlements and of correcting and supplementing earlier geographical information. Partly through its use new islands, identified by such modern names as Air Force, Prince Charles, Borden, Meighen, and Mackenzie King, began to appear on maps. The largest single undertaking was an airborne geological survey of the entire Canadian Arctic completed by the government in the 1950's. The launching of Anik, Canada's telecommunications satellite, in 1972 made it possible to link all northern settlements in a communications network.

LEGEND

Centre of activity.................... •
Northern Administration Office............ ●
R.C.M.P. Office (where agent for Northern Administration)............ □
School................................ ▲
Northern Canada Power Commission, power station . ⅏
Airport............................... ○
Emergency airport..................... ○
Scheduled air services.................
Non-scheduled air services...........
Highways.............................
    (under construction).............
Sea Routes............................

Note: Almost all of Canada is now covered by definitive (vertical) air photography. The Queen Elizabeth Islands and part of Banks and Victoria Islands are covered by exploratory air photography, a combination of vertical and oblique.

Place-names in blue are names of recent interest in the north.

KILOMETRES

RECENT DEVELOPMENTS

LEGEND

COMMUNICATIONS

Main railways (transcontinental and northern) —+—+—+—
Northern highways..................................
St. Lawrence Seaway..................................| | | | | |

RESOURCES AND DEVELOPMENT

Main agricultural areas..................................
Main forest areas..................................
Minerals

Metal mines..................................●
Coal mines..................................■
Non-metallic minerals (asbestos, potash)..................................▲

Oil and gas fields..................................⬭
Pipelines..................................- - - - -
Smelters and refineries (major)..................................▥
Major hydro developments..................................

INDUSTRY

Manufacturing centres
10 000 - 24 000 workers..................................●
25 000 - 75 000 workers..................................▲
250 000 - 300 000 workers..................................■

100   0   100   200   300   400   500

KILOMETRES

117 Economic Development

In the early twentieth century agriculture was the dominant economic activity in Canada. The towns, cities and transportation facilities, which owed their existence to agriculture, were concentrated in the south where climate and soils were favourable to farming. Subsequent years have seen little expansion of agricultural settlement with the notable exception of the Peace River country which was settled in the 1920's and 1930's.

The rapid growth of manufacturing during and after the First World War further strengthened the dominant position of the South in the economic life of the country. The populated areas of Southern Quebec and Southern Ontario enjoyed an early advantage in manufacturing and continued to attract large numbers of new industries. Montreal and Toronto became the leading centres of manufacturing activity. In the West, Vancouver and Winnipeg, strategically located on transportation routes, developed into important manufacturing centres. Alberta promises to become a major area of manufacturing as it begins to capitalize on its energy resources.

As the demand for raw materials increased, the huge expanse of Canada's north began to receive more attention. The development of the area was based largely on the exploitation of lumber and mineral resources. The great metal belt from Sudbury to Cobalt was an especially valued part of the 'Old North' of the 1920's. The opening of Norman Wells oil field in 1920 and the discovery of pitchblende at Port Radium in 1930 were milestones in the economic development of the farther north.

In recent years there has been a growing awareness of the problems created by the development of northern resources, especially those affecting the environment and the rights of the native peoples. In January 1967 Yellowknife was named capital of the Northwest Territories, in a step intended to bring the territorial government closer to the people. In its 1969–70 session the Canadian parliament passed the Arctic Waters Pollution Prevention Act.

RECENT DEVELOPMENTS

118 Continental Defence and NATO

In addition to mineral discoveries, continental defence requirements were responsible for much of the attention paid to northern Canada after the Second World War. In this period world power was centred round two great nuclei, the United States and Russia, and attack by the latter across the North Pole rapidly became feasible through the development of long-range bombers and later intercontinental ballistic missiles. Being in the direct line of any such attack, Canada's defence role took on an entirely new character. The North Atlantic Treaty Organization, which Canada had helped form in 1949 along with the United States, Britain, and a number of western European countries, mainly with a view to the defence of the latter, now had to be supplemented by increasing emphasis on defence of the North American continent itself. Among the steps taken for this purpose was the construction in Canada of three lines of radar stations to give advance warning of an enemy air attack. The first, the Pinetree Line, became fully operational in 1954 and consisted of thirty-four stations, twenty-two built in the United States. It was followed by the McGill Fence or Mid-Canada Line undertaken by Canada, and finally by the American-financed Distant Early Warning Line, in use by 1957. In order to consolidate the defence of North America, the North American Air Defence Command (Norad) was established in 1957. As emphasis shifted increasingly to defence against ballistic missiles, other early warning systems were added in the farther north and along the east and west coasts.

In March 1965, the Mid-Canada Line ceased operations because improvements to the Pinetree Line radar stations had reduced its usefulness.

LEGEND

NATO countries . . . .
Warsaw Pact countries . . . .
Other communist countries . . . .

MALDIVE IS.
(INDIA)

SRI LANKA · Colombo

NICOBAR IS. (INDIA)

Djakarta

SINGAPORE

BRUNEI

MALAYSIA

S. VIETNAM

CAMBODIA

THAILAND

N. VIETNAM

LAOS

HONG KONG

Manila

PHILIPPINES

INDONESIA

NEW GUINEA

PAPUA AND NEW GUINEA (AUSTRALIA)

AUSTRALIA

Canberra · Melbourne

Sydney

SOLOMON IS.

NEW HEBRIDES

NAURU

NORFOLK I.

NEW ZEALAND

Wellington

40°

20°

FIJI ISLANDS

KERMADEC IS. (N.Z.)

CHATHAM IS. (N.Z.)

ELLICE IS.

TONGA IS.

WESTERN SAMOA

TOKELAU IS.

GILBERT IS.

0°

20°

40°

COOK IS. (N.Z.)

HAWAIIAN ISLANDS

Honolulu

60°

80°

ANDAMAN IS. (INDIA)

Krung Thep

Rangoon

BURMA

BANGLADESH

INDIA

NEPAL

Calcutta

New Delhi

INDIA

Bombay

Karachi

PAKISTAN

AFGHANISTAN

KASHMIR

Lhasa

CHINA

Peking

UNION OF SOVIET SOCIALIST REPUBLICS

Mos

Lenin

FINLA

JAPAN

Tokyo

GREENLAND

ALASKA

Juneau

CANADA

Ottawa

Vancouver

UNITED STATES

OF

AMERICA

San Francisco

Chicago

Los Angeles

New Orleans

MEXICO

Mexico City

BELIZE

160°

140°

120°

100°

80°

·PITCAIRN I.

LEGEND

Independent countries of Commonwealth

Principal insular territories, dependencies, colonies and protectorates

GHANA

GILBERT IS.

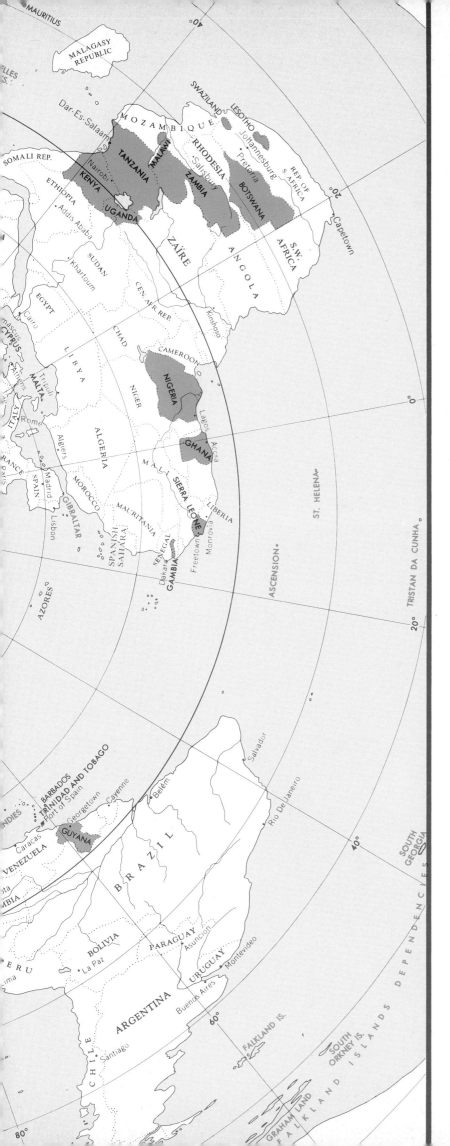

Canada's new military commitments in NATO – and directly with the United States – were not the only features of her growing participation in world affairs after the Second World War. Having become an independent nation within the Commonwealth following the passage of the Statute of Westminster in 1931, Canada continued to have special, though increasingly intangible, ties with Britain and the older Dominions, and developed new ties with many former British colonies in Asia and Africa which became independent members of the Commonwealth after the Second World War.

In 1950 Canada joined with Britain and the older Dominions in a program to aid the newly independent nations of India, Pakistan and Ceylon (Sri Lanka). This program, known as the Colombo Plan, was subsequently broadened to include an area from Afghanistan to Indonesia. As more countries emerged from colonial rule Canada initiated new programs of aid involving the Commonwealth Caribbean (1958), Commonwealth Africa (1959), Francophone Africa (1962), and Latin America (1964). The inclusion of non-Commonwealth countries as aid recipients reflected Canada's increasingly independent position in the world. As a partly French-speaking country it seemed appropriate that Canada should make available technical assistance to former colonies of France and Belgium. The inclusion of Latin America in her aid program was indicative of Canada's commitment to the Western Hemisphere.

In 1972–73 Canada provided a total of over $300 000 000 in aid to the following regions: Asia (51%), Francophone Africa (18%), Commonwealth Africa (16%), Commonwealth Caribbean (4%), Latin America (4%) and other programs (7%). In addition, Canada provided development assistance to the Third World through international institutions and non-governmental organizations. Much of this effort was channelled through various agencies of the United Nations, an organization which Canada joined at its founding on June 26, 1945.

RECENT DEVELOPMENTS

Part 6 Economic and Political Trends, 1871-1971

On these pages will be found a wealth of information on the economic and political development of Canada since Confederation. While the various graphs and charts may be used independently of the rest of the book, it will be helpful to relate them to earlier sections, for example:

Population — pages 50, 53, 66
Settlement & Communications — pages 48-9, 51, 64-5, 66
Internal Boundaries — pages 55, 67
Resource Development — pages 46-7, 52-3, 70, 77, 78-9, and particularly 80-81.
Costs of War — page 76

In order to offset the distortion of dolla▮ values by inflation, all value graphs hav▮ been shown in both current and constar▮ (1935-39 = 100) dollars. Thus trends, which this Part is designed to show, a▮ more accurately portrayed.

Unless otherwise stated, all information is from Statistics Canada.

POPULATION

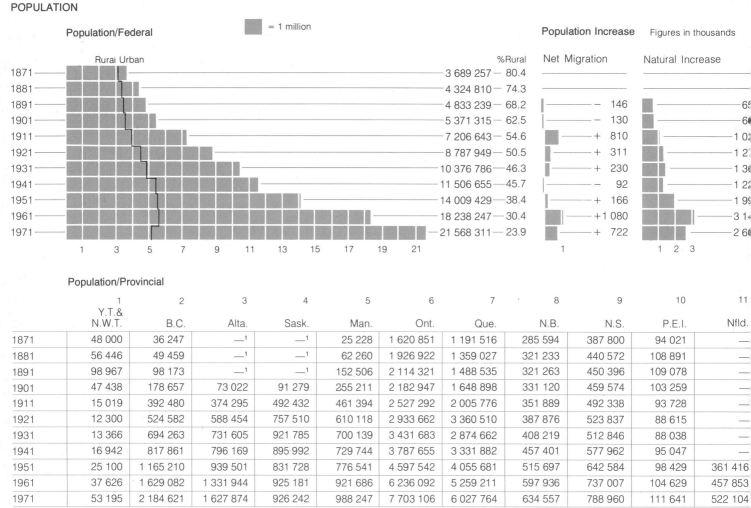

Population/Federal

= 1 million

Population Increase   Figures in thousands

Net Migration   Natural Increase

Year	%Rural	Net Migration	Natural Increase
1871	3 689 257 — 80.4		
1881	4 324 810 — 74.3		
1891	4 833 239 — 68.2	− 146	6▮
1901	5 371 315 — 62.5	− 130	6▮
1911	7 206 643 — 54.6	+ 810	1 0▮
1921	8 787 949 — 50.5	+ 311	1 2▮
1931	10 376 786 — 46.3	+ 230	1 3▮
1941	11 506 655 — 45.7	− 92	1 2▮
1951	14 009 429 — 38.4	+ 166	1 9▮
1961	18 238 247 — 30.4	+1 080	3 1▮
1971	21 568 311 — 23.9	+ 722	2 6▮

Population/Provincial

	1 Y.T. & N.W.T.	2 B.C.	3 Alta.	4 Sask.	5 Man.	6 Ont.	7 Que.	8 N.B.	9 N.S.	10 P.E.I.	11 Nfld.
1871	48 000	36 247	—¹	—¹	25 228	1 620 851	1 191 516	285 594	387 800	94 021	—
1881	56 446	49 459	—¹	—¹	62 260	1 926 922	1 359 027	321 233	440 572	108 891	—
1891	98 967	98 173	—¹	—¹	152 506	2 114 321	1 488 535	321 263	450 396	109 078	—
1901	47 438	178 657	73 022	91 279	255 211	2 182 947	1 648 898	331 120	459 574	103 259	—
1911	15 019	392 480	374 295	492 432	461 394	2 527 292	2 005 776	351 889	492 338	93 728	—
1921	12 300	524 582	588 454	757 510	610 118	2 933 662	3 360 510	387 876	523 837	88 615	—
1931	13 366	694 263	731 605	921 785	700 139	3 431 683	2 874 662	408 219	512 846	88 038	—
1941	16 942	817 861	796 169	895 992	729 744	3 787 655	3 331 882	457 401	577 962	95 047	—
1951	25 100	1 165 210	939 501	831 728	776 541	4 597 542	4 055 681	515 697	642 584	98 429	361 416
1961	37 626	1 629 082	1 331 944	925 181	921 686	6 236 092	5 259 211	597 936	737 007	104 629	457 853
1971	53 195	2 184 621	1 627 874	926 242	988 247	7 703 106	6 027 764	634 557	788 960	111 641	522 104

¹Included in N.W.T.

= 1 million

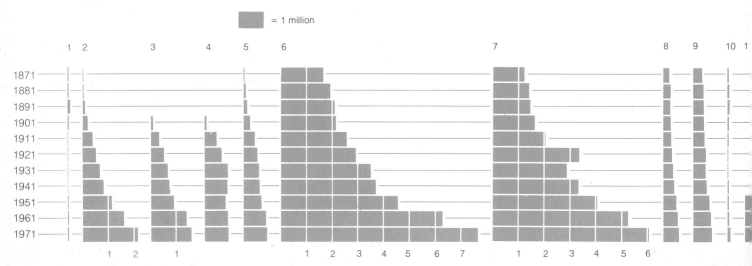

National Origin

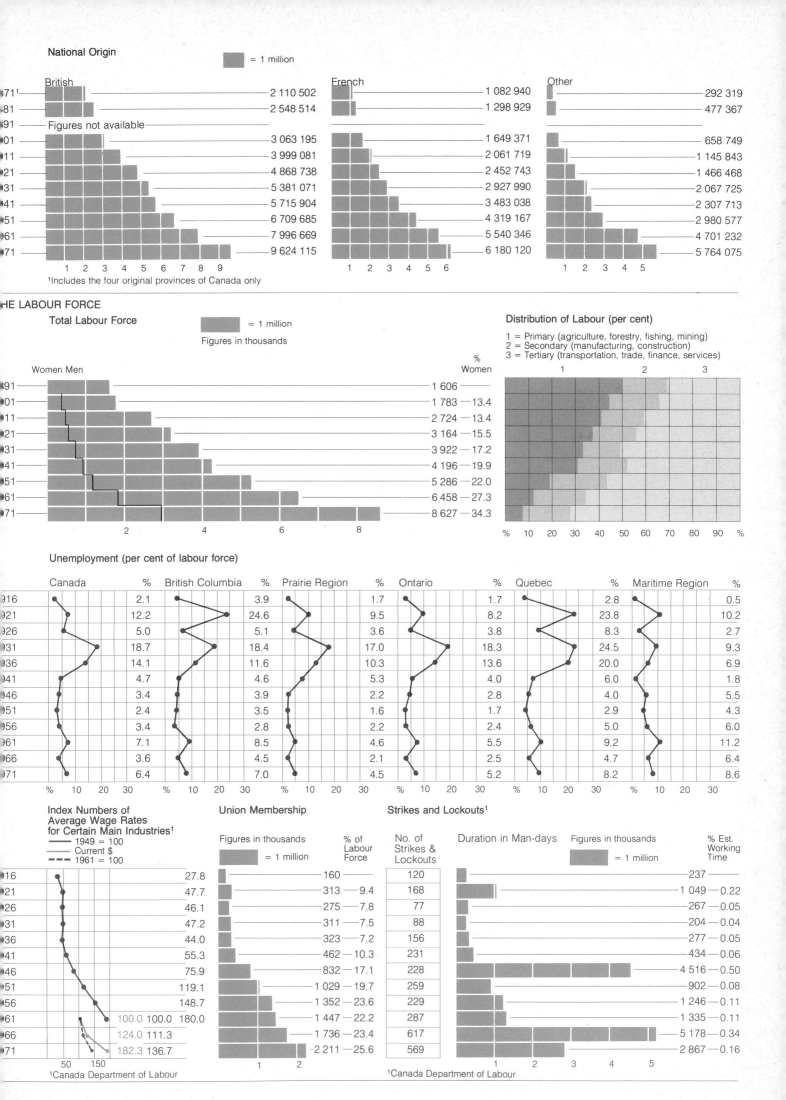

= 1 million

British
Year	
1871[1]	2 110 502
1881	2 548 514
1891	Figures not available
1901	3 063 195
1911	3 999 081
1921	4 868 738
1931	5 381 071
1941	5 715 904
1951	6 709 685
1961	7 996 669
1971	9 624 115

1 2 3 4 5 6 7 8 9

[1]Includes the four original provinces of Canada only

French
Year	
1871	1 082 940
1881	1 298 929
1901	1 649 371
1911	2 061 719
1921	2 452 743
1931	2 927 990
1941	3 483 038
1951	4 319 167
1961	5 540 346
1971	6 180 120

1 2 3 4 5 6

Other
Year	
1871	292 319
1881	477 367
1901	658 749
1911	1 145 843
1921	1 466 468
1931	2 067 725
1941	2 307 713
1951	2 980 577
1961	4 701 232
1971	5 764 075

1 2 3 4 5

THE LABOUR FORCE

Total Labour Force

= 1 million
Figures in thousands

Year	Women Men	% Women
1891		1 606
1901		1 783 — 13.4
1911		2 724 — 13.4
1921		3 164 — 15.5
1931		3 922 — 17.2
1941		4 196 — 19.9
1951		5 286 — 22.0
1961		6 458 — 27.3
1971		8 627 — 34.3

2 4 6 8

Distribution of Labour (per cent)

1 = Primary (agriculture, forestry, fishing, mining)
2 = Secondary (manufacturing, construction)
3 = Tertiary (transportation, trade, finance, services)

% 10 20 30 40 50 60 70 80 90 %

Unemployment (per cent of labour force)

	Canada %	British Columbia %	Prairie Region %	Ontario %	Quebec %	Maritime Region %
1916	2.1	3.9	1.7	1.7	2.8	0.5
1921	12.2	24.6	9.5	8.2	23.8	10.2
1926	5.0	5.1	3.6	3.8	8.3	2.7
1931	18.7	18.4	17.0	18.3	24.5	9.3
1936	14.1	11.6	10.3	13.6	20.0	6.9
1941	4.7	4.6	5.3	4.0	6.0	1.8
1946	3.4	3.9	2.2	2.8	4.0	5.5
1951	2.4	3.5	1.6	1.7	2.9	4.3
1956	3.4	2.8	2.2	2.4	5.0	6.0
1961	7.1	8.5	4.6	5.5	9.2	11.2
1966	3.6	4.5	2.1	2.5	4.7	6.4
1971	6.4	7.0	4.5	5.2	8.2	8.6

% 10 20 30 (repeated for each region)

Index Numbers of Average Wage Rates for Certain Main Industries[1]

—— 1949 = 100
—— Current $
- - - 1961 = 100

Year	
1916	27.8
1921	47.7
1926	46.1
1931	47.2
1936	44.0
1941	55.3
1946	75.9
1951	119.1
1956	148.7
1961	100.0 100.0 180.0
1966	124.0 111.3
1971	182.3 136.7

50 150

[1]Canada Department of Labour

Union Membership

Figures in thousands
= 1 million

Year	Figures	% of Labour Force
1916	160	
1921	313	9.4
1926	275	7.8
1931	311	7.5
1936	323	7.2
1941	462	10.3
1946	832	17.1
1951	1 029	19.7
1956	1 352	23.6
1961	1 447	22.2
1966	1 736	23.4
1971	2 211	25.6

1 2

Strikes and Lockouts[1]

Duration in Man-days Figures in thousands
= 1 million

Year	No. of Strikes & Lockouts	Duration	% Est. Working Time
1916	120	237	
1921	168	1 049	0.22
1926	77	267	0.05
1931	88	204	0.04
1936	156	277	0.05
1941	231	434	0.06
1946	228	4 516	0.50
1951	259	902	0.08
1956	229	1 246	0.11
1961	287	1 335	0.11
1966	617	5 178	0.34
1971	569	2 867	0.16

1 2 3 4 5

[1]Canada Department of Labour

GROSS NATIONAL PRODUCT

⌐ = Constant $ (1935-39 = 100)

Current $ / Constant

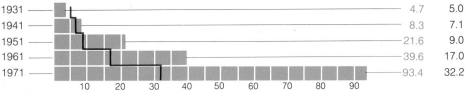

Gross National Product ($ billions)[1]

Year		GNP	Per Capita ($)		
1931		4.7	5.0	453	482
1941		8.3	7.1	724	622
1951		21.6	9.0	1 545	643
1961		39.6	17.0	2 113	906
1971		93.4	32.2	4 331	1 494

Total Gross Fixed Capital Formation ($ billions)[1]

Year	Value	
1931	0.8	0.
1941	1.5	1.
1951	4.7	3.
1961	8.2	3.
1971	20.5	7.

[1]Gross national product is the total value of goods and services produced in a given period by Canadian residents. Canadian residents include both individuals and institutions such as government agencies, corporations, and non-profit institutions, which are normally resident in Canada.

Total gross fixed capital formation is the gross expenditure by both business and government on new, durable assets, such as buildings, highways, and equipment

---

AGRICULTURE

Total Number of Farms
● = 100,000 farms
Figures in thousands

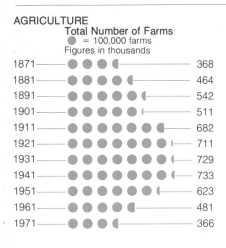

Year	Farms
1871	368
1881	464
1891	542
1901	511
1911	682
1921	711
1931	729
1941	733
1951	623
1961	481
1971	366

Occupied Agricultural Land (million acres)[1]

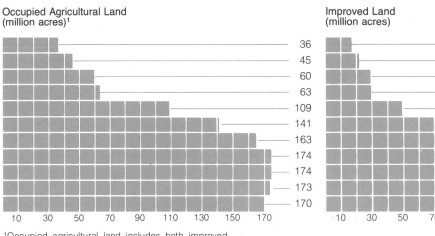

Year	Occupied	Improved Land (million acres)
1871	36	1
1881	45	2
1891	60	2
1901	63	3
1911	109	4
1921	141	7
1931	163	8
1941	174	9
1951	174	9
1961	173	10
1971	170	10

[1]Occupied agricultural land includes both improved land and uncultivated areas such as woodland.

Agricultural Production

⌐ = Constant $ (1935-39 = 100)

Current $ / Constant

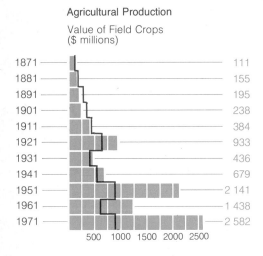
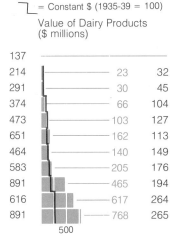

Value of Field Crops ($ millions) / Value of Dairy Products ($ millions) / Farmers' Cash Income from Farm Products ($ millions)[1]

Year	Field Crops	Dairy 1	Dairy 2	Farmers' 1	Farmers' 2
1871	111	137			
1881	155	214	23	32	
1891	195	291	30	45	
1901	238	374	66	104	
1911	384	473	103	127	
1921	933	651	162	113	
1931	436	464	140	149	472	50
1941	679	583	205	176	876	75
1951	2 141	891	465	194	2 725	1 13
1961	1 438	616	617	264	2 888	1 23
1971	2 582	891	768	265	4 495	1 55

[1]Without supplementary payments

Wheat Production

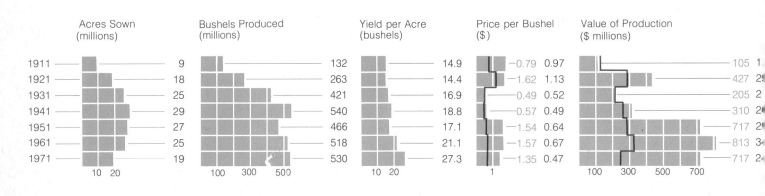

Acres Sown (millions) / Bushels Produced (millions) / Yield per Acre (bushels) / Price per Bushel ($) / Value of Production ($ millions)

Year	Acres Sown	Bushels Produced	Yield per Acre	Price per Bushel		Value of Production	
1911	9	132	14.9	0.79	0.97	105	1
1921	18	263	14.4	1.62	1.13	427	2
1931	25	421	16.9	0.49	0.52	205	2
1941	29	540	18.8	0.57	0.49	310	2
1951	27	466	17.1	1.54	0.64	717	2
1961	25	518	21.1	1.57	0.67	813	3
1971	19	530	27.3	1.35	0.47	717	2

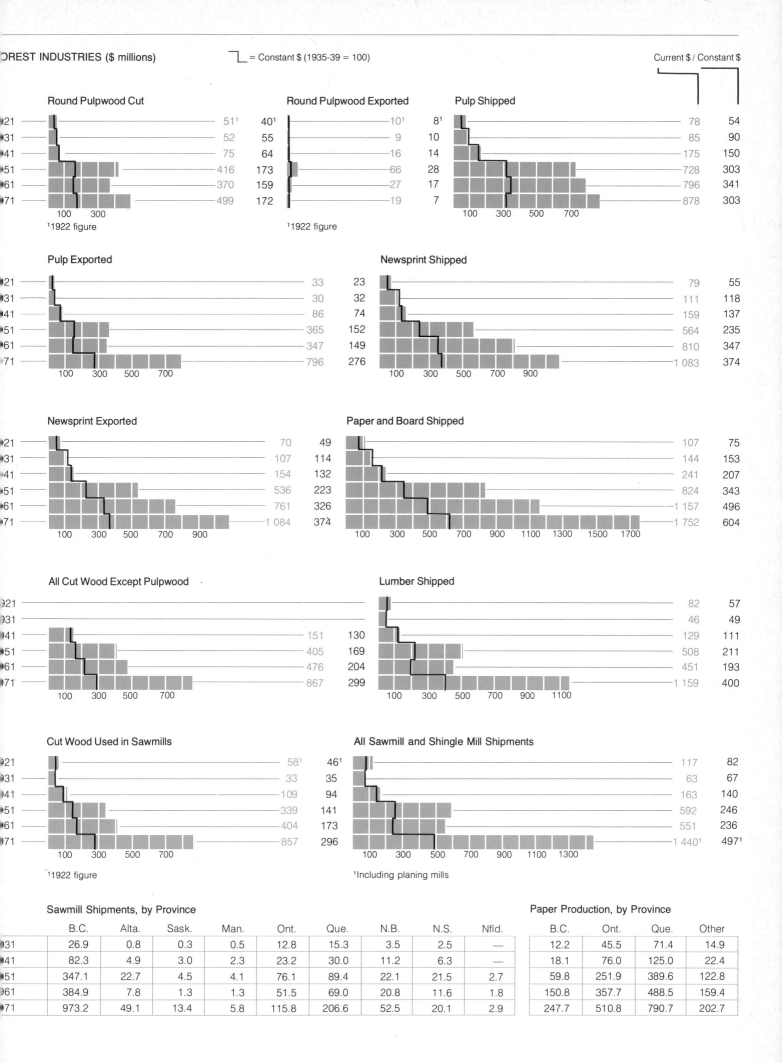

Round Pulpwood Cut

'21	51[1]	40[1]
'31	52	55
'41	75	64
'51	416	173
'61	370	159
'71	499	172

100   300

[1]1922 figure

Round Pulpwood Exported

'21	10[1]	8[1]
'31	9	10
'41	16	14
'51	66	28
'61	27	17
'71	19	7

[1]1922 figure

Pulp Shipped

'21	78	54
'31	85	90
'41	175	150
'51	728	303
'61	796	341
'71	878	303

100   300   500   700

Pulp Exported

'21	33	23
'31	30	32
'41	86	74
'51	365	152
'61	347	149
'71	796	276

100   300   500   700

Newsprint Shipped

'21	79	55
'31	111	118
'41	159	137
'51	564	235
'61	810	347
'71	1 083	374

100   300   500   700   900

Newsprint Exported

'21	70	49
'31	107	114
'41	154	132
'51	536	223
'61	761	326
'71	1 084	374

100   300   500   700   900

Paper and Board Shipped

'21	107	75
'31	144	153
'41	241	207
'51	824	343
'61	1 157	496
'71	1 752	604

100   300   500   700   900   1100   1300   1500   1700

All Cut Wood Except Pulpwood

'21		
'31		
'41	151	130
'51	405	169
'61	476	204
'71	867	299

100   300   500   700

Lumber Shipped

'21	82	57
'31	46	49
'41	129	111
'51	508	211
'61	451	193
'71	1 159	400

100   300   500   700   900   1100

Cut Wood Used in Sawmills

'21	58[1]	46[1]
'31	33	35
'41	109	94
'51	339	141
'61	404	173
'71	857	296

100   300   500   700

[1]1922 figure

All Sawmill and Shingle Mill Shipments

'21	117	82
'31	63	67
'41	163	140
'51	592	246
'61	551	236
'71	1 440[1]	497[1]

100   300   500   700   900   1100   1300

[1]Including planing mills

Sawmill Shipments, by Province

	B.C.	Alta.	Sask.	Man.	Ont.	Que.	N.B.	N.S.	Nfld.
'31	26.9	0.8	0.3	0.5	12.8	15.3	3.5	2.5	—
'41	82.3	4.9	3.0	2.3	23.2	30.0	11.2	6.3	—
'51	347.1	22.7	4.5	4.1	76.1	89.4	22.1	21.5	2.7
'61	384.9	7.8	1.3	1.3	51.5	69.0	20.8	11.6	1.8
'71	973.2	49.1	13.4	5.8	115.8	206.6	52.5	20.1	2.9

Paper Production, by Province

	B.C.	Ont.	Que.	Other
'31	12.2	45.5	71.4	14.9
'41	18.1	76.0	125.0	22.4
'51	59.8	251.9	389.6	122.8
'61	150.8	357.7	488.5	159.4
'71	247.7	510.8	790.7	202.7

FISHERIES ($ millions)

⌐ = Constant $ (1935-39 = 100)

Current $ / Constant

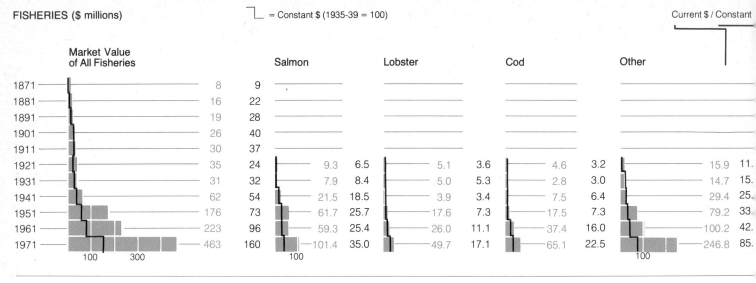

	Market Value of All Fisheries			Salmon			Lobster			Cod			Other		
1871			8	9											
1881			16	22											
1891			19	28											
1901			26	40											
1911			30	37											
1921			35	24	9.3	6.5	5.1	3.6	4.6	3.2	15.9	11.			
1931			31	32	7.9	8.4	5.0	5.3	2.8	3.0	14.7	15.			
1941			62	54	21.5	18.5	3.9	3.4	7.5	6.4	29.4	25.			
1951			176	73	61.7	25.7	17.6	7.3	17.5	7.3	79.2	33.			
1961			223	96	59.3	25.4	26.0	11.1	37.4	16.0	100.2	42.			
1971			463	160	101.4	35.0	49.7	17.1	65.1	22.5	246.8	85.			

100   300   100   100

MINING ($ millions)

⌐ = Constant $ (1935-39 = 100)

Current $ / Constant

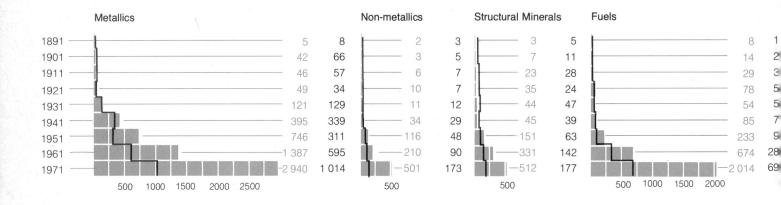

Value of All Mineral Production

		Current $	Constant
1886		10	1
1891		19	2
1901		66	10
1911		103	12
1921		172	12
1931		230	24
1941		560	48
1951		1 245	51
1961		2 603	1 11
1971		5 968	2 05

500 1000 1500 2000 2500 3000 3500 4000 4500 5000 5500

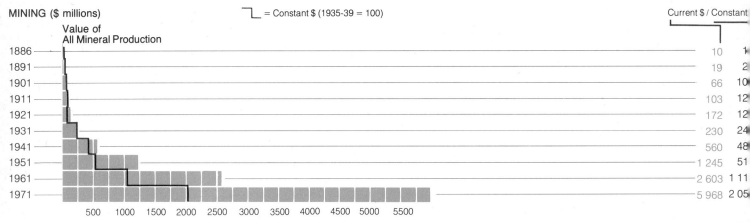

	Metallics		Non-metallics		Structural Minerals		Fuels	
1891	5	8	2	3	3	5	8	1
1901	42	66	3	5	7	11	14	2
1911	46	57	6	7	23	28	29	3
1921	49	34	10	7	35	24	78	5
1931	121	129	11	12	44	47	54	5
1941	395	339	34	29	45	39	85	7
1951	746	311	116	48	151	63	233	9
1961	1 387	595	210	90	331	142	674	28
1971	2 940	1 014	501	173	512	177	2 014	69

500 1000 1500 2000 2500   500   500   500 1000 1500 2000

Production of Selected Minerals

Year	Metallics								Non-metallics	Fuels				Structural Mineral	
	Copper	Gold	Iron Ore	Lead	Nickel	Silver	Uranium	Zinc	Asbestos	Coal	Natural Gas	Nat. Gas By-prods.	Petroleum Crude	Cement	Sand & Gravel
1886	0.4	1.5	0.1	—	—	0.3	—	—	0.2	3.7	—	—	0.5	0.1	—
1891	1.2	0.9	0.1	—	2.4	0.4	—	—	1.0	7.0	0.2	—	1.0	0.1	0.1
1901	6.1	24.1	—	2.2	4.6	3.3	—	—	1.3	12.7	0.3	—	1.0	0.7	0.1
1911	6.9	9.8	0.5	0.8	10.2	17.4	—	0.1	2.9	26.5	1.9	—	0.4	7.6	0.4
1921	6.0	19.1	0.2	3.8	6.8	8.5	—	2.5	4.9	72.5	4.6	—	0.6	14.2	2.5
1931	24.1	58.1	—	7.3	15.3	6.1	—	6.1	4.8	41.2	9.0	—	4.2	15.8	6.7
1941	64.4	205.8	1.4	15.5	68.7	8.3	0.9	17.5	21.5	58.1	12.7	—	14.4	13.1	10.4
1951	149.0	161.9	31.1	58.2	151.3	21.9	26.4[1]	135.8	81.6	109.0	7.2	—	116.7	40.4	44.6
1961	255.2	158.6	188.0	47.1	351.3	29.6	195.7	104.8	129.0	70.1	68.4	27.3	487.6	103.9	104.7
1971	760.0	79.9	555.1	109.5	800.1	71.8	50.2[2]	418.2	204.0	121.7	342.5	193.2	1 356.9	191.2	152.6

[1] 1954 figure   [2] 1970 figure

= $1 billion Current
= $1 billion Constant (1935-39 = 100)
All figures in millions

Current $ / Constant $

Gross Value of Manufacturers

Year	Current	Constant
1871	222	273
1881	310	428
1891	470	700
1901	481	755
1911	1 166	1 438
1921	2 489	1 736
1931	2 555	2 718
1941	6 076	5 220
1951	16 392	6 824
1961	23 439	10 047
1971	50 276	17 343

Net Value of Manufactures

Year	Current	Constant
1871	97	119
1881	130	180
1891	219	326
1901	215	338
1911	564	695
1921	1 124	784
1931	1 252	1 332
1941	2 605	2 238
1951	6 941	2 890
1961	10 435	4 473
1971	21 738	7 498

Gross Value of Manufactures, by Province ($ millions)

	Y.T. & N.W.T.	B.C.	Alta.	Sask.	Man.	Ont.	Que.	N.B.	N.S.	P.E.I.	Nfld.
1921	—	144.2	58.6	40.5	103.1	1 307.3	731.4	55.0	72.8	3.9	—
1931	—	162.5	62.6	39.2	110.0	1 257.5	801.6	51.8	66.0	3.4	—
1941	0.3	413.0	142.7	96.0	211.5	3 121.8	1 841.1	111.4	133.9	4.6	—
1951	2.0	1 404.9	458.3	250.8	551.3	8 074.7	4 916.2	307.1	303.6	22.5	100.6
1961	3.4	1 927.0	935.5	331.9	716.7	11 563.7	7 022.2	390.6	381.4	30.6	135.9
1971	7.7	4 236.0	2 080.6	578.0	1 344.9	26 270.6	13 833.2	806.8	798.2	58.0	261.9

Gross Value of Leading Manufactures ($ millions)

1891
Food products — 76
Timber & lumber — 73
Textiles — 55
Iron & steel products — 29
Leather & its products — 24

1901
Food products — 125
Timber & lumber — 80
Textiles — 67
Iron & steel products — 35
Leather & its products — 35

1920
Food products — 977
Textiles — 468
Timber & lumber — 403
Iron & steel products — 389
Paper & printing — 312

1941
Non-ferrous metal smelting & refining — 379
Pulp & paper — 334
Slaughtering & meat-packing — 296
Motor vehicles — 280
Butter & cheese — 180
Electrical supplies — 178

1961
Pulp & paper — 1 635
Smelting & refining — 1 471
Petroleum refining — 1 184
Slaughtering & meat-packing — 1 081
Motor vehicles — 871
Iron & steel — 789

1970
Motor vehicles — 2 963
Pulp & paper — 2 851
Slaughtering & meat-packing — 2 061
Petroleum refining — 1 759
Iron & steel products — 1 692
Dairy products — 1 369

CONSTRUCTION

⌐ = Constant $ (1935-39 = 100)

Current $ / Constant

Construction Contracts Awarded ($ millions)¹

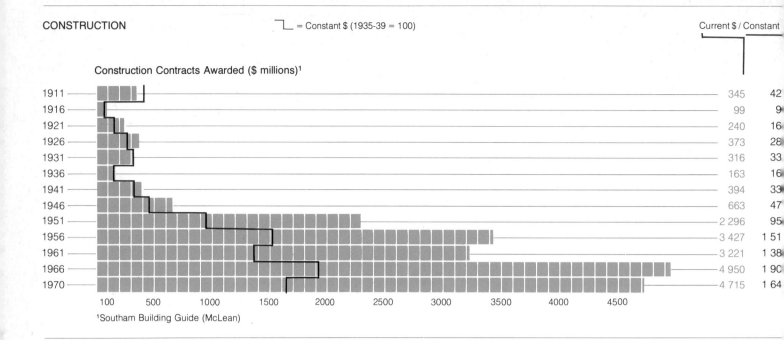

Year	$ millions	
1911	345	42
1916	99	9
1921	240	16
1926	373	28
1931	316	33
1936	163	16
1941	394	33
1946	663	47
1951	2 296	95
1956	3 427	1 51
1961	3 221	1 38
1966	4 950	1 90
1970	4 715	1 64

¹Southam Building Guide (McLean)

ELECTRIC POWER

Generator Capacity (million kW)

Year	million kW
1921	1
1931	4
1941	6
1951	9
1961	24
1971	46

Net Electric Power Generated (billion kWh)

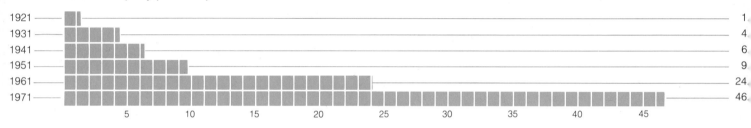

Year	Total	Hydraulic	Thermal
1926	12.1	11.9	0.
1931	16.3	16.0	0.
1941	33.3	32.6	0.
1951	54.9	53.0	1.
1961	113.7	103.9	9.
1971	215.1	160.5	54.

Electric Power Generated, by Province (billion kWh)

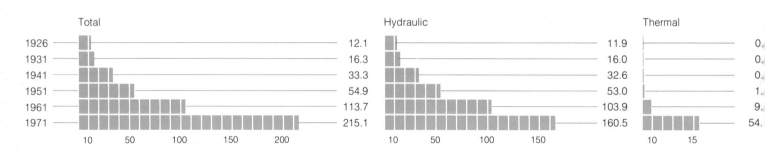

	Y.T. & N.W.T.	B.C.	Alta.	Sask.	Man.	Ont.	Que.	N.B.	N.S.	P.E.I.	Nfld.
1921	—	0.5	0.1	0.05	0.3	2.8	1.8	0.03	0.03	0.001	—
1931	—	1.2	0.2	0.1	1.1	4.9	8.1	0.4	0.3	0.004	—
1941	—	2.5	0.3	0.2	1.9	9.6	17.7	0.5	0.5	0.01	—
1951	0.06	2.7	1.0	1.0	2.6	16.0	29.7	0.8	0.9	0.03	0.2
1961	0.2	13.2	3.8	2.5	3.8	35.0	49.9	1.9	1.9	0.09	1.5
1971	0.5	29.0	11.1	6.1	9.7	68.1	76.2	5.7	4.1	0.3	5.0

Telegraph Pole Kilometres (thousands)

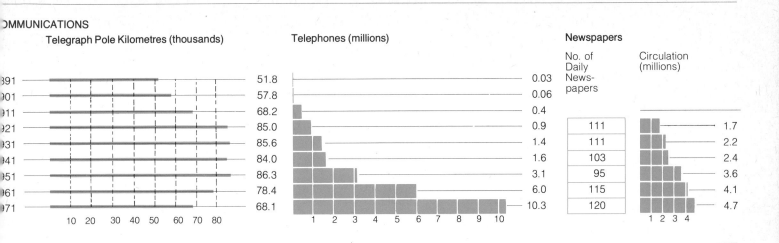

	Telegraph Pole Kilometres (thousands)	Telephones (millions)	Newspapers No. of Daily Newspapers	Circulation (millions)
891		51.8	0.03	
901		57.8	0.06	
911		68.2	0.4	
921		85.0	0.9	111	1.7
931		85.6	1.4	111	2.2
941		84.0	1.6	103	2.4
951		86.3	3.1	95	3.6
961		78.4	6.0	115	4.1
971		68.1	10.3	120	4.7

Telegraph scale: 10 20 30 40 50 60 70 80
Telephones scale: 1 2 3 4 5 6 7 8 9 10
Circulation scale: 1 2 3 4

RANSPORTATION

Railways

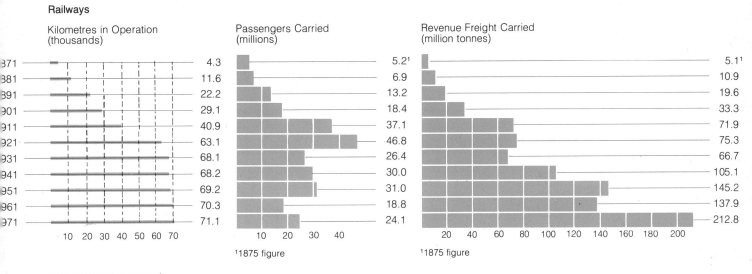

	Kilometres in Operation (thousands)	Passengers Carried (millions)	Revenue Freight Carried (million tonnes)
871	4.3	5.2[1]	5.1[1]
881	11.6	6.9	10.9
891	22.2	13.2	19.6
901	29.1	18.4	33.3
911	40.9	37.1	71.9
921	63.1	46.8	75.3
931	68.1	26.4	66.7
941	68.2	30.0	105.1
951	69.2	31.0	145.2
961	70.3	18.8	137.9
971	71.1	24.1	212.8

Kilometres scale: 10 20 30 40 50 60 70
Passengers scale: 10 20 30 40
[1] 1875 figure
Revenue Freight scale: 20 40 60 80 100 120 140 160 180 200
[1] 1875 figure

Shipping (million tonnes)

	Freight Shipped Through Canals	International Seaborne Freight Loaded	Unloaded
891	2.6		
901	5.1		
911	34.2		
921	8.5	7.9	3.2
931	14.6	9.7	7.0
941	21.2	14.7	26.7
951	26.4	24.6	34.5
961	51.5	48.4	35.3
971	108.2	93.3	54.4

Canals scale: 20 40 60 80 100
Loaded scale: 20 40 60 80
Unloaded scale: 20 40

Road Transportation

Highways (thousand km)

Number of Vehicles Registered

= 1 million   Figures in thousands

Air Transportation

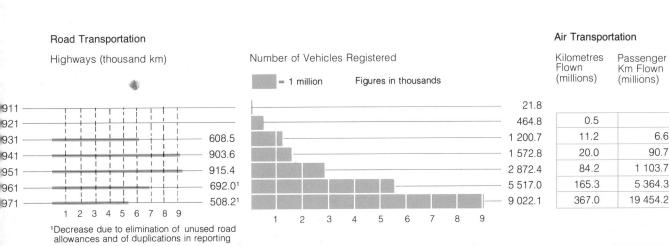

	Highways (thousand km)	Number of Vehicles Registered	Kilometres Flown (millions)	Passenger Km Flown (millions)	Freight Carried (million kg)
911		21.8			
921		464.8	0.5		0.04
931	608.5	1 200.7	11.2	6.6	1.1
941	903.6	1 572.8	20.0	90.7	7.5
951	915.4	2 872.4	84.2	1 103.7	26.6
961	692.0[1]	5 517.0	165.3	5 364.3	95.0
971	508.2[1]	9 022.1	367.0	19 454.2	332.7

Highways scale: 1 2 3 4 5 6 7 8 9
Vehicles scale: 1 2 3 4 5 6 7 8 9

[1] Decrease due to elimination of unused road allowances and of duplications in reporting

FOREIGN TRADE

All figures in millions ■ = $1 billion ⌐ = Constant $ (1935-39 = 100) Current $ / Constant $

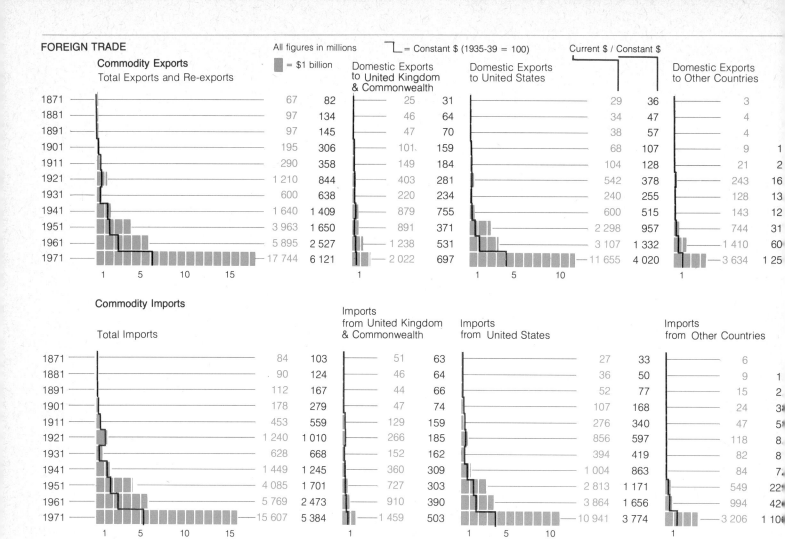

Commodity Exports

Year	Total Exports and Re-exports (Current)	(Constant)	Domestic Exports to United Kingdom & Commonwealth (Current)	(Constant)	Domestic Exports to United States (Current)	(Constant)	Domestic Exports to Other Countries (Current)	(Constant)
1871	67	82	25	31	29	36	3	
1881	97	134	46	64	34	47	4	
1891	97	145	47	70	38	57	4	
1901	195	306	101	159	68	107	9	1
1911	290	358	149	184	104	128	21	2
1921	1 210	844	403	281	542	378	243	16
1931	600	638	220	234	240	255	128	13
1941	1 640	1 409	879	755	600	515	143	12
1951	3 963	1 650	891	371	2 298	957	744	31
1961	5 895	2 527	1 238	531	3 107	1 332	1 410	60
1971	17 744	6 121	2 022	697	11 655	4 020	3 634	1 25

Commodity Imports

Year	Total Imports (Current)	(Constant)	Imports from United Kingdom & Commonwealth (Current)	(Constant)	Imports from United States (Current)	(Constant)	Imports from Other Countries (Current)	(Constant)
1871	84	103	51	63	27	33	6	
1881	90	124	46	64	36	50	9	1
1891	112	167	44	66	52	77	15	2
1901	178	279	47	74	107	168	24	3
1911	453	559	129	159	276	340	47	5
1921	1 240	1 010	266	185	856	597	118	8
1931	628	668	152	162	394	419	82	8
1941	1 449	1 245	360	309	1 004	863	84	7
1951	4 085	1 701	727	303	2 813	1 171	549	22
1961	5 769	2 473	910	390	3 864	1 656	994	42
1971	15 607	5 384	1 459	503	10 941	3 774	3 206	1 10

BALANCE OF INTERNATIONAL PAYMENTS ($ millions)

Current Account / Capital Account

	Current Account							Capital Account		
	Mdse. Exports	Other Receipts	Total Receipts	Mdse. Imports	Other Payments	Total Payments	Current Account Balance	Direct Foreign Investment in Canada	Other Capital Transactions	Net Capital Balance
1930	880	417	1 297	973	661	1 634	− 337			+ 373
1935	732	420	1 152	526	501	1 027	+ 125			− 123
1940	1 202	597	1 799	1 006	642	1 648	+ 151			− 148
1945	3 474	1 012	4 486	1 442	2 355	3 797	+ 689			− 21
1950	3 139	1 145	4 284	3 132	1 471	4 603	− 319	+225	+816	+1 041
1955	4 332	1 594	5 926	4 543	2 070	6 613	− 689	+445	+198	+ 643
1960	5 392	1 823	7 215	5 540	2 908	8 448	−1 233	+670	+524	+1 194
1965	8 745	2 903	11 648	8 627	4 151	12 778	−1 130	+535	+753	+1 288
1970	16 751	5 125	21 876	13 845	6 995	20 840	+1 036	+835	−341	+ 494

FOREIGN OWNERSHIP

Estimates of Foreign Capital Invested in Canada

Figures in millions ■ = $1 billion ⌐ = Constant $ (1935-39 = 100) Current $ / Constant $

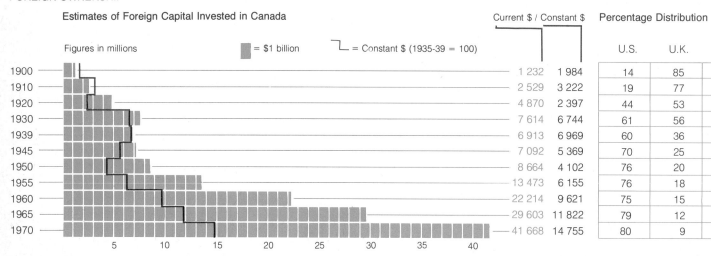

Year	Current $	Constant $	Percentage Distribution U.S.	U.K.	Other
1900	1 232	1 984	14	85	1
1910	2 529	3 222	19	77	4
1920	4 870	2 397	44	53	3
1930	7 614	6 744	61	36	3
1939	6 913	6 969	60	36	4
1945	7 092	5 369	70	25	5
1950	8 664	4 102	76	20	4
1955	13 473	6 155	76	18	6
1960	22 214	9 621	75	15	10
1965	29 603	11 822	79	12	9
1970	41 668	14 755	80	9	11

Figures in millions ■ = $1 billion ⌝ = Constant $ (1935-39 = 100) Current $ / Constant $

Federal Revenue

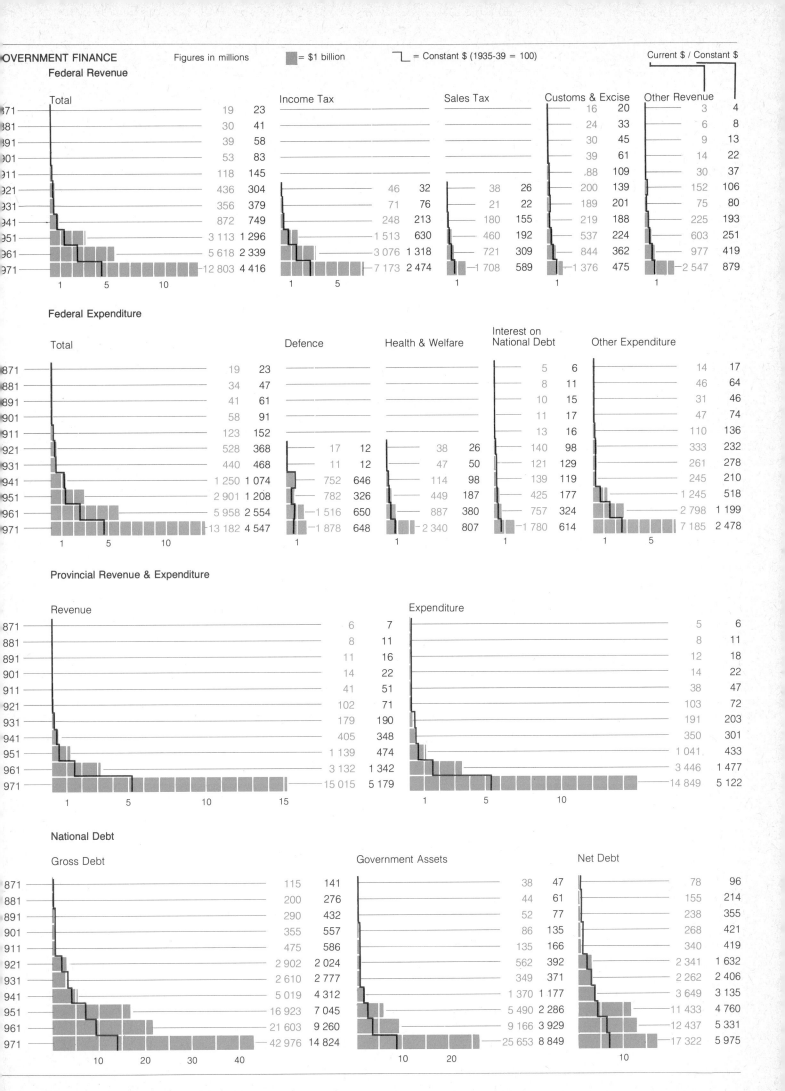

Total

1871	19 23
1881	30 41
1891	39 58
1901	53 83
1911	118 145
1921	436 304
1931	356 379
1941	872 749
1951	3 113 1 296
1961	5 618 2 339
1971	12 803 4 416

Income Tax

1921	46 32
1931	71 76
1941	248 213
1951	1 513 630
1961	3 076 1 318
1971	7 173 2 474

Sales Tax

1921	38 26
1931	21 22
1941	180 155
1951	460 192
1961	721 309
1971	1 708 589

Customs & Excise

1871	16 20
1881	24 33
1891	30 45
1901	39 61
1911	88 109
1921	200 139
1931	189 201
1941	219 188
1951	537 224
1961	844 362
1971	1 376 475

Other Revenue

1871	3 4
1881	6 8
1891	9 13
1901	14 22
1911	30 37
1921	152 106
1931	75 80
1941	225 193
1951	603 251
1961	977 419
1971	2 547 879

Federal Expenditure

Total

1871	19 23
1881	34 47
1891	41 61
1901	58 91
1911	123 152
1921	528 368
1931	440 468
1941	1 250 1 074
1951	2 901 1 208
1961	5 958 2 554
1971	13 182 4 547

Defence

1921	17 12
1931	11 12
1941	752 646
1951	782 326
1961	1 516 650
1971	1 878 648

Health & Welfare

1921	38 26
1931	47 50
1941	114 98
1951	449 187
1961	887 380
1971	2 340 807

Interest on National Debt

1871	5 6
1881	8 11
1891	10 15
1901	11 17
1911	13 16
1921	140 98
1931	121 129
1941	139 119
1951	425 177
1961	757 324
1971	1 780 614

Other Expenditure

1871	14 17
1881	46 64
1891	31 46
1901	47 74
1911	110 136
1921	333 232
1931	261 278
1941	245 210
1951	1 245 518
1961	2 798 1 199
1971	7 185 2 478

Provincial Revenue & Expenditure

Revenue

1871	6 7
1881	8 11
1891	11 16
1901	14 22
1911	41 51
1921	102 71
1931	179 190
1941	405 348
1951	1 139 474
1961	3 132 1 342
1971	15 015 5 179

Expenditure

1871	5 6
1881	8 11
1891	12 18
1901	14 22
1911	38 47
1921	103 72
1931	191 203
1941	350 301
1951	1 041 433
1961	3 446 1 477
1971	14 849 5 122

National Debt

Gross Debt

1871	115 141
1881	200 276
1891	290 432
1901	355 557
1911	475 586
1921	2 902 2 024
1931	2 610 2 777
1941	5 019 4 312
1951	16 923 7 045
1961	21 603 9 260
1971	42 976 14 824

Government Assets

1871	38 47
1881	44 61
1891	52 77
1901	86 135
1911	135 166
1921	562 392
1931	349 371
1941	1 370 1 177
1951	5 490 2 286
1961	9 166 3 929
1971	25 653 8 849

Net Debt

1871	78 96
1881	155 214
1891	238 355
1901	268 421
1911	340 419
1921	2 341 1 632
1931	2 262 2 406
1941	3 649 3 135
1951	11 433 4 760
1961	12 437 5 331
1971	17 322 5 975

Federal Election Results

Election year	Liberal	Conservative*	Unionist	Progressive	Liberal Progressive	United Farmers	C.C.F./N.D.P.**	Social Credit	Ralliement Créditiste	Independent & Others	Total Seats	Nfld.	P.E.I.	N.S.	N.B.	Que.	Ont.	Man.	Sask.	Alta.	N.W.T.	Y.T.	B.C.	Prime Minister	Reigning Sovereign	Governor General
1867	80	101									181			19	15	65	82							1867 Sir John A. Macdonald		1867 Viscount Monck / 1868 Lord Lisgar
1872	97	103									200			21	16	65	88	4					6	1873 Alexander Mackenzie		1872 Earl of Dufferin
1874	133	73									206		6	21	16	65	88	4					6			
1878	69	137									206		6	21	16	65	88	4					6	1878 Sir John A. Macdonald	Victoria	1878 Marquis of Lorne
1882	71	139									210		6	21	16	65	91	5					6			1883 Marquis of Lansdowne
1887	92	123									215		6	21	16	65	92	5		4			6			1888 Lord Stanley of Preston
1891	92	123									215		6	21	16	65	92	5		4			6	1891 Sir John Abbott / 1892 Sir John Thompson / 1894 Sir MacKenzie Bowell		1893 Earl of Aberdeen
1896	117	89								7	213		5	20	14	65	92	7		4			6	1896 Sir Charles Tupper / 1896 Sir Wilfrid Laurier		1898 Earl of Minto
1900	133	80									213		5	20	14	65	92	7		4			6		1901	
1904	139	75									214		4	18	13	65	86	10	10			1	7		Edward VII	1904 Earl Grey
1908	133	85								3	221		4	18	13	65	86	10	10	7		1	7		1910	
1911	86	133								2	221		4	18	13	65	86	10	10	7		1	7	1911 Sir Robert Borden		1911 Duke of Connaught
1917	82		153								235		4	16	11	65	82	15	16	12		1	13	1920 Arthur Meighen	George V	1916 Duke of Devonshire
1921	117	50		64						4	235		4	16	11	65	82	15	16	12		1	13	1921 W. L. Mackenzie King		1921 Lord Byng of Vimy
1925	101	116		24						4	245		4	14	11	65	82	17	21	16		1	14			
1926	116	91		13	9	11				5	245		4	14	11	65	82	17	21	16		1	14	1926 Arthur Meighen / 1926 W. L. Mackenzie King		1926 Viscount Willingdon
1930	88	137		2	3	10				5	245		4	14	11	65	82	17	21	16		1	14	1930 R.B. Bennett		1931 Earl of Bessborough
1935	171	39			2		7	17		9	245		4	12	10	65	82	17	21	17		1	16	1935 W.L. Mackenzie King	1936 Edw. VIII 1936	1935 Lord Tweedsmuir
1940	178	39			3		8	10		7	245		4	12	10	65	82	17	21	17		1	16		George VI	1940 Earl of Athlone
1945	125	67					28	13		12	245		4	12	10	65	82	17	21	17		1	16	1948 Louis S. St. Laurent		1945 Viscount Alexander
1949	190	41					13	10		8	262	7	4	13	10	73	83	16	20	17		1	18			
1953	170	51					23	15		6	265	7	4	12	10	75	85	14	17	17	1	1	22		1952	1952 Vincent Massey
1957	105	112					25	19		4	265	7	4	12	10	75	85	14	17	17	1	1	22	1957 John G. Diefenbaker		
1958	48	208					8			1	265	7	4	12	10	75	85	14	17	17	1	1	22			
1962	99	116					19	30		1	265	7	4	12	10	75	85	14	17	17	1	1	22			1959 Georges P. Vanier
1963	129	95					17	24			265	7	4	12	10	75	85	14	17	17	1	1	22	1963 Lester B. Pearson	Elizabeth II	
1965	131	97					21	5	9	2	265	7	4	12	10	75	85	14	17	17	1	1	22			
1968	155	72					22		14	1	264	7	4	11	10	74	88	13	13	19	1	1	23	1968 Pierre Elliott Trudeau		1967 Roland Michener
1972	109	107					31	15		2	264	7	4	11	10	74	88	13	13	19	1	1	23			
1974	141	95					16		11	1	264	7	4	11	10	74	88	13	13	19	1	1	23			1974 Jules Léger

* From 1945 on, called Progressive Conservative

** Cooperative Commonwealth Federation; beginning 1962 New Democratic Party

SELECTED BIBLIOGRAPHY

In addition to works listed below, the following periodicals contain valuable articles: *The Beaver*, *The Canadian Geographical Journal*, The Canadian Historical Association's *Annual Report*, the *Canadian Historical Review*, and the *Canadian Journal of Economics and Political Science*.

General Works

Brebner, J. Bartlett/*Canada: A Modern History*/ The University of Michigan History of the Modern World/Ann Arbor, 1960

Canada/Department of Mines and Technical Surveys/*National Atlas of Canada*/Ottawa, 1974

————/Statistics Canada/*Canada Year Books*/ Ottawa, 1905–1973

————/Statistics Canada/*Censuses of Canada, 1871, 1881, 1891, 1901, 1911, 1921, 1931, 1941, 1951, 1961, 1971*/Ottawa

Easterbrook, W. T. and H. G. J. Aitken/ *Canadian Economic History*/Toronto, 1956

Glazebrook, G. P. de T./*History of Transportation in Canada*/Carleton Library, 11 and 12/Toronto, 1964

Harris, R. C. and J. Warkentin/*Canada Before Confederation*/New York, 1974

Kirwan, L. P./*The White Road: A Survey of Polar Exploration from the Vikings to Fuchs*/ London, 1959

Lower, A. R. M./*Colony to Nation*/2nd ed./ Toronto, 1957

Mackintosh, W. A. and W. L. G. Joerg, eds./ *Canadian Frontiers of Settlement*/9 vols./ Toronto, 1934–38

Morton, W. L./*The Kingdom of Canada: A General History from Earliest Times*/Toronto, 1963

Wade, Mason/*The French Canadian Outlook: A Brief Account of the Unknown North Americans*/Carleton Library, 14/Toronto, 1964

————/*The French Canadians, 1760–1945*/ Toronto, 1955

Warkentin, John, ed./*The Western Interior of Canada: A Record of Geographical Discovery, 1612–1917*/Carleton Library, 15/Toronto, 1964

Exploration and Development to 1763

Biggar, H. P./*The Works of Samuel de Champlain*/Champlain Society/6 vols./Toronto, 1922–36

————/*The Voyages of Jacques Cartier: published from the originals with translations, notes, and appendices*/Ottawa, 1924

Brebner, J. B./*New England's Outpost: Acadia before the Conquest of Canada*/New York, 1927

————/*The Explorers of North America, 1492–1806*/Anchor Book ed./Garden City, 1955

Burt, A. L./*Sixteenth Century Maps Relating to Canada: a check-list and bibliography*/Ottawa, 1956

Clark, A. H./*Acadia: The Geography of Early Nova Scotia to 1760*/Madison, 1969

Crouse, N. M./*La Vérendrye, Fur Trader and Explorer*/Toronto, 1956

Doughty, A. G. and C. Martin, eds./*The Kelsey Papers*/Ottawa, 1929

Eccles, W. J./*The Canadian Frontier: 1534–1760*/ New York, 1969

Ganong, W. F./*Crucial Maps in the Early Cartography and Place-Nomenclature of the Atlantic Coast of Canada*/Royal Society of Canada, Special Publications, 7/Toronto, 1964

Harris, R. C./*The Seigneurial System in Early Canada*/Madison, 1966

Hoffman, Bernard G./*Cabot to Cartier: Sources of a Historical Ethnography of North-eastern North America, 1497–1550*/ Toronto, 1961

Innis, H. A./*The Fur Trade in Canada*/2nd ed./ Toronto, 1956

Jenness, D./*The Indians of Canada*/3rd ed./ Ottawa, 1955

Mealing, S. R., ed./*The Jesuit Relations and Allied Documents: A Selection*/Carleton Library, 7/Toronto, 1963

Morrison, S. E./*The European Discovery of America: The Northern Voyages, A.D. 500–1600*/New York, 1971

Oleson, Tryggvi J./*Early Voyages and Northern Approaches, 1000–1632*/Toronto, 1964

Stefansson, V., ed./*The Three Voyages of Martin Frobisher*/2 vols./London, 1938

Trudel, Marcel/*Histoire de la Nouvelle-France*. I. *Les Vaines Tentatives, 1524–1603*/Montréal et Paris, 1963

————/*An Atlas of New France*/Quebec, 1968

Wagner, H. R./*The Cartography of the North West Coast of America to the Year 1800*/ 2 vols./Berkeley, 1937

British North America, 1763-1867

Anderson, Bern/*Surveyor of the Sea: The Life and Voyages of Captain George Vancouver*/ Toronto, 1960

Cowan, Helen I./*British Emigration to British North America*/Revised and enlarged edition/ Toronto, 1961

Craig, Gerald, M./*Upper Canada: The Formative Years, 1784–1841*/Toronto, 1963

Creighton, Donald G./*The Empire of the St. Lawrence*/Toronto, 1956

Dunham, Aileen/*Political Unrest in Upper Canada, 1815–1836*/Carleton Library, 10/ Toronto, 1963

Gray, John Morgan/*Lord Selkirk of Red River*/ Toronto, 1963

Hansen, M. L. and J. B. Brebner/*The Mingling of the Canadian and American Peoples*/New Haven, 1940

Hind, H. J./*Narrative of the Canadian Red River Exploring Expedition of 1857, and of the Assiniboine and Saskatchewan Exploring Expedition of 1858*/2 vols./London, 1860

Lamb, W. Kaye, ed./*The Letters and Journals of Simon Fraser, 1806–1808*/Toronto, 1960

Landon, F./*Western Ontario and the American Frontier*/Carleton Library, 34/Toronto, 1967

Lower, A. R. M./*The North American Assault on the Canadian Forest*/New Haven, 1936

Mackenzie, A./*Voyages from Montreal, on the River St. Lawrence, through the Continent of North America, to the Frozen and Pacific Oceans, in the years 1789 and 1793*/London, 1801

MacNutt, W. S./*The Atlantic Provinces: The Emergence of Colonial Society, 1712–1857*/ Toronto, 1965

Morton, A. S./*History of the Canadian West to 1870–71*/Toronto, 1939

Morton, W. L./*Manitoba, A History*/Toronto, 1957

Nicholson, N. L./*The Boundaries of Canada, its Provinces and Territories*/Ottawa, 1954

Ormsby, Margaret A./*British Columbia: A History*/Toronto, 1958

Ouellet, F./*Histoire Economique et Sociale du Québec, 1760–1850*/Montréal, 1966

Paterson, G. C./*Land Settlement in Upper Canada*/Toronto, 1921

Rich, E. E./*The History of the Hudson's Bay Company, 1670–1870*/London, 1958–59

————/*The Fur Trade and the North-west to 1857*/ Toronto, 1967

Ross, E./*Beyond the River and the Bay*/Toronto, 1970

Spelt, J./*Urban Development in South-Central Ontario*/Assen, 1955

Spry, Irene M./*The Palliser Expedition: An Account of John Palliser's British North American Exploring Expedition, 1857–1860*/ Toronto, 1964

Tyrrell, J. B., ed./*David Thompson's Narrative of his Explorations in Western America 1784–1812*/Toronto, 1916

United Kingdom/*The Journals, Detailed Reports and Observations Relative to the Exploration by Captain Palliser of that Portion of British North America . . . between the Western Shore of Lake Superior and the Pacific Ocean during the Years 1857, 1858, 1859, and 1860*/London, 1863

Vancouver, J., ed./*A Voyage of Discovery to the North Pacific Ocean . . . under the Command of Captain George Vancouver*/3 vols./London, 1798

Wright, E. C./*The Loyalists of New Brunswick*/ Ottawa, 1955

Zaslow, Morris, ed./*The Defended Border: Upper Canada and the War of 1812*/Toronto, 1964

Founding a Nation, 1867-1914

Hedges, J. B./*Building the Canadian West: The Land and Colonization Policies of the Canadian Pacific Railways*/New York, 1939

Innis, H. A. and A. R. M. Lower/*Settlement of the Forest and Mining Frontiers*/Toronto, 1936

Mackintosh, W. A./*Prairie Settlement: The Geographic Setting*/Toronto, 1934

Morton, A. S. and C. Martin/*History of Prairie Settlement and Dominion Lands Policy*/ Toronto, 1938

Stanley, G. F. G./*The Birth of Western Canada: A History of the Riel Rebellions*/Toronto, 1961

————/*Louis Riel*/Toronto, 1963

Taylor, A./*Geographical Discovery and Exploration in the Queen Elizabeth Islands*/ Ottawa, 1955

Warkentin, J. and R. Ruggles/*Manitoba Historical Atlas*/Historical and Scientific Society of Manitoba, 1970

Wright, J. F. C./*Saskatchewan, the History of a Province*/Toronto, 1955

Wars and Expansion since 1914

Glazebrook, G. P. de T./*A History of Canadian External Relations*/Toronto, 1950

Mackay, R. A., ed./*Newfoundland: Economic, Diplomatic, and Strategic Studies*/Toronto, 1946

Nicholson, G. W. L./*Canadian Expeditionary Force 1914–1919: The Official History of the Canadian Army in the First World War*/ Ottawa, 1962

————/*Official History of the Canadian Army in the Second World War*. II. *The Canadians in Italy, 1943–45*/Ottawa, 1956

Schull, Joseph/*The Far Distant Ships. An Official Account of Canadian Naval Operations in the Second World War*/Ottawa, 1952

Stacey, C. P./*The Canadian Army, 1939–1945*/ Ottawa, 1948

————/*An Official History of the Canadian Army in the Second World War*. I. *Six Years of War: the Army in Canada, Britain and the Pacific*. III. *The Victory Campaign, The Operations in North-West Europe, 1944–1945*/ Ottawa, 1955, 1960

Tucker, G. N./*The Naval Service of Canada: Its Official History*. I. *Origins and Early Years*. II. *Activities on Shore during the Second World War*/Ottawa, 1952

INDEX

P

Pacific Coast exploration, 41–42, *41–42*
Palliser, John, *41*, 60
Palliser's 'Triangle', 41, 60, *60*
Paris, Treaty of (1763), *21*, 30, *30–31*, 34
Paris, Treaty of (1783), 34, *34*, 53
Paris, Treaty of (1815), 54, *54*
Parry, Sir William, 41, *41*
Passamaquoddy Bay, 40, *40*
Passchendaele, Belgium, 71, *71*
Peace River, 2, 41, 43, 80, *81*
Peary, Robert E., 68, *69*
Pelee Island, 51
Pembina, 56
Pennsylvania Loyalists, 37
Percé, Isle, 17, 19
Pérez, Juan, 41, *41*
Petroleum. *See* Oil.
Philadelphia, *33*
Piegan Indians, 12
Pigeon Hill, P.Q., 51
Pigeon River, 45
Pinetree Network, 82–83, *83*
Placentia, Nfld., 22
Plains Cree Indians, 12
Plattsburg, Battle of, 39, *39*
Pleistocene Age, 2
Po River, *73*
Population statistics, 24, *25*, 48–50, 53, 66, 86–87
Porcupine River, 2, *70*
Portage de Traite, *44*, 45.
   See also Frog Portage.
Portage La Loche, *44*, 45.
   See also Methye Portage.
Portage la Prairie, 56
Port Arthur, Ont., 56, *56*, 64, 65.
   See also Prince Arthur's Landing, Thunder Bay
Port aux Basques, Nfld., 77, *77*
Port Hope, Lindsay, and Beaverton Railway, 51
Portland, Me., 46, 49
Portland Canal, 70
Portland Point, 24
Port Radium, 78, 80, *81*
Port Roseway. *See* Shelburne, N.S.
Port Royal, 17, 19, 22, *22*, 24, *25*.
   See also Annapolis Royal.
Potawatomi Indians, 13.
   See also Ojibwa Indians.
Poundmaker, *58*, 59
Prairie du Chien, 38, *39*
Prairie Provinces, 56, *56*, 64, *64*
   administration, 67, 67
   boundaries, 31–32, *32*, 34, 34–35, 40, *40*, 55, *55*, 67, *67*
   exploration, 20, *21*, 41, *41*
   Indians, 12–13, 57, *57*, 59
   land survey, 62–63, *62–63*
   mining, 80, *81*
   physical conditions, 41, 60, 60–61
   settlement, 60–66, *60–64*, *66*
   trade, *44*, 45–46, *47*
Prescott, Ont., 39, 51, *51*
Prevost, Sir George, *39*
Prideaux, John, 26
Prince Albert, Sask., *58*, 59
Prince Arthur's Landing, 56, *56*.
   See also Port Arthur.
Prince Charles Island, 79, *79*
Prince Edward Island, 22, 24, 27, 30–32, *30–32*, 34, 40, 55, 65
   agriculture, *25*, 52, *52*
   exploration, 8–11, 17, 19
   fisheries, 52
   land question, *32*, 55, *55*
   population, *36*, 37
   trade, 47.
   See also Isle St. Jean and St. John Island.
Prince Edward Island Railway, 55, *55*, 64, 65
Prince George, B.C., 80
Prince of Wales Regiment, 37
Prince Rupert, B.C., 64, *64*, 80
Princeton, B.C., 43
Proclamation of 1763, 31, *31*, 54, *54*
Provincial revenue and expenditure, 95
Put-in-Bay, Battle of, 38, *39*

Q

Quadra, Juan Francisco de la Bodega y, 41, *41*
Quebec Act (1774), 32, *32*, 54, *54*, *67*
Quebec (city), 9, *9*, 17, 18, *21*, 24, *25*, 26, *27–28*, 28–29, 31, 33, *33*, 36, *36*, 46
   See also Stadacona.
Quebec, Province of (1763–91, 1867–1971), 33, *33*, 65, 79
   agriculture, 94–95
   boundaries, 31–32, *31–32*, 34–35, *34–35*, 54–55, *54–55*, 67, *67*, 77
   mining, 80-81, *81*
   See also New France and Lower Canada.
Quebec-Labrador Boundary Dispute, 31–32, *31–32*, 54, *54*, 67, *67*
Queen Anne's War, *22*
Queen Charlotte Islands, 43, *43*
Queen's Rangers, 37
Queenston Heights, 38, *39*
Quesnel, B.C., 43
Quieunonascaran, 16
Quirpon Island, 40, *40*, 54

R

Radisson, Pierre Esprit, *21*
Rae, John, 41, *41*
Railways, 59, *60*, 80–81, *81*
   land grants, 62–63, *62–63*
   Lower and Upper Canada, 46–49, *49*, 51
   Maritimes before 1867, 52–53, *53*, 55, *55*
   Newfoundland, 77, *77*
   statistics, 93
   transcontinental, 55, *55*, *58*, 58–59, 62–65, *64*.
   See also individual railway names.
Rainy Lake, 34, *34*, 45
Rainy Lake Fort, 45
Ramea Islands, 40, *40*, 54
Rapide Plat Canal, 65
Rat Portage (Kenora), 56
Rebellions of 1837–8, 51, *51*
Reciprocity Treaty (1854), 54, *54*
Red Deer River, 62
Red River, 20, 44, 56, *56*, 63
   Insurrection, 56, *56*
   settlement, 44, *44*, 56, *56*.
   See also Manitoba.
   trails, 56
Regina, Sask., 59, 67, *67*, 102
Resolute, N.W.T., 78, 80, 82
Rhine River, 74–75, *75*
Richardson, Sir John, 41, *41*
Richelieu River, *16*, 26, *26–27*
Riche Point, 22, *22*, 31–32, 34, *34*, 54
Rideau Canal, 46, 48, 65
Ridgeway, Battle of, 51, *51*
Riel, Louis, *56*, 58
Rivière du Loup, 46
Roads, 43, 48–49, *49*, 52, 52–53, 56, 80
   statistics, 93
Roberval, Jean François de la Roque, Sieur de, *9*
Rocky Mountains, 2, 20, *21*, 43, *43*, 45, 62, *62–63*
Rocky Mountain House, 45
Rome-Berlin Axis, 72, *73*
Rosario Strait, 43
Rouyn, P.Q., *81*
Royal Canadian Air Force, 72, *73*, 76
Royal Canadian Navy, 72, *73*, 76
Royal Fencible Americans, 37
Rupert House, 46
Rupert's Land, 12, *22*, 22–23, *30–32*, 30–35, 40, *44*, 45, 48–49, *55*, 62, *66*, *67*.
   See also Hudson's Bay Company.
Rush, Richard, *40*
Rush-Bagot Agreement (1818), *40*
Russia, 42–43, *42–43*, 45
Rut, John, 8, *9*
Ruysch, Johannes, *7*

S

Sackets Harbor, 39
Saguenay, Kingdom of, *9*, 11
Saguenay River, 17, 19
St. Albans, Vt., 51
St. Andrews and Quebec Railway, 52
Ste. Anne, 24.
   See also Fredericton, N.B.
St. Boniface, Man., 56
St. Charles, Lower Canada, 51
St. Charles River, 28
St. Croix River, 34, *34–35*, 40, *40*
St. Denis, Lower Canada, 51, *51*
St. Eloi, Belgium, 71, *71*
St. Eustache, Lower Canada, 51, *51*
Ste. Foy, Battle of, 26, *27*
St. Ignace, 16.
   See also Scanonaenrat.
St. Jean, Isle. *See* Isle St. Jean.
St. John, Lake, 31, *31*
Saint John, N.B., 24, 37, 47, 52
St. John Island, 31–32, *31–32*, *36*, 37.
   See also Isle St. Jean and Prince Edward Island.
St. John River, N.B., 17, 19, *36*, 37
St. John River, P.Q., 31, *31*, 54, *54*
St. Johns, P.Q., 33, *33*, 39.
   See also Fort St. Jean.
St. John's, Newfoundland, 22, 47, 53, 77, *77*
St. Joseph I, 16
St. Joseph II, 16
St. Lawrence, Gulf of, *9*, 11
St. Lawrence and Atlantic Railway, 48–49
St. Lawrence and Ottawa Railway, 48–49, 51
St. Lawrence River, *9*, 9–11, *12*, *16*, 16–19, 40, *40*, 46–47, *47*
   seaway, 81
   waterway, *64*, 65
St. Lawrence Valley, 24, *25*
St. Leger, Barry, 33, *33*
Ste. Marie I, 16
Ste. Marie II, 16
St. Maurice River, *25*
St. Paul, Minn., 46, 56
St. Pierre and Miquelon, *30*, 30–31, 34, *34*, 54, *54*, 77
St. Roch, R.C.M.P. Schooner, 78–79, *79*
St. Simon, Paul Denis de, 20
St. Thomas, Ont., 48, 51
Salish Indians, Interior, 12
Sanctuary Wood, Belgium, 71
San Ildefonso, Treaty of (1762), *30*
San Juan boundary dispute, 43, *43*
San Juan Island, 43
Saratoga, Battle of, 33
Sarcee Indians, 12
Sarnia, Ont., 48, 51
Saskatchewan, District of, 67, *67*
Saskatchewan, Province of, 66–67, *67*
   boundaries, 67, *67*
   mining, 80
   population, 66
Saskatchewan River, 20, 41, *44*, 45
Sauk Indians, 13
Sault Ste. Marie, Ont., 20, 48
Sault Ste. Marie Canal, 65
Saunders, Admiral Sir Charles, 26–27, *27*, *28*
Savanne Portage, 45
Sawmill Bay, N.W.T., 78
Scanonaenrat, 16.
   See also St. Ignace.
Schefferville, P.Q., 77, 81
Scheldt River, 74–75, *75*
Scott, Thomas, 56
Seigneurial grants, 24–25, *25*, 48–49, *49*
Sekani Indians, 12
Selkirk, Thomas Douglas, fifth Earl of, *44*
Selkirk grant, 40, 45
Selkirk settlers, *62*
Seneca Indians, 13
Sept-Iles, P.Q., 77, 81
Settlement:
   Acadia, 24, *25*

British Columbia, 43, *43* 66, *66*
   Maritimes, 24, *25*, *36–37*, 37, 52–53, *52–53*, 55
   Newfoundland, *36*, 37, 52–53
   Prairie Provinces, 60–66, *60–64*, 66
   St. Lawrence region, 24–25, *25*, 36, *36–37*, 48–49, *49*, 50, *50*
Seven Oaks, Battle of, 44
Seven Years' War, 26–27, *26–27*
Shelburne, N.S., *36*, 37
Sherbrooke, Sir John Coape, *39*
Shipbuilding, 52, *52*
Sicilian Campaign, 73, *73*
Silver, 80–81
Simcoe, Lake, 16
Simpson, Thomas, 41, *41*
Sioux Indians, 21
Six Nations Reserve, 36
Skagway, Alaska, 70, *70*, 80
Slave Indians, 12
Smallwood Reservoir, 77
Snow, John A., 56
Snow road, 56
Somme, Battle of the, 71, *71*
Somme River, 71, 75
Sorel, Lower Canada, 36, *36–37*
Soulanges Canal, 65
South Beveland, Netherlands, 75
South Branch House, 45
South Saskatchewan River, 62, 62–63
Spanish America, 43, *43*
Spanish Succession, War of (Queen Anne's War), 22
Spence's Bridge, B.C., 43
Spokane Houses, 45
Stadacona, *9*, 9–10.
   See also Quebec (city).
Steep Rock Lake, 80
Stefansson, Vilhjalmur, 68, *69*
Stephanius, Sigurdius, *3*
Stephenville, Nfld., 82
Stikine River, 43, *43*, 70, *70*
Stikine Territory, 43, *43*
Stoney Creek, Battle of, 38, *39*
Strange, Maj.-Gen. T. B., *58*, 59
Stratford, Ont., 48, 51
Submarine cable, 52–53
Sudbury, Ont., 80, *81*
Superior, Lake, 20–21, 32, 34–35, 40, *40*, 58, *58*
Sverdrup, Otto, 68, *69*
Swift Current, *58*, 59
Sydney, N.S., 37

T

Tadoussac, 17, 19–20
Taglish Indians, 12
Tahltan Indians, 12
Talbot, Thomas, 49
Talbot roads, 48
Talbot settlement, 48
Talon, Jean, *21*, 25
Tanana River, 2
Teanaustayé, 16.
   See also St. Joseph II.
Tecumseh, *39*
Telegraph services, 52–53, *58*, 59
Temiscouata, Lake, 53, *53*
Temiscouata Road, 53
Thames River, Battle of the (Moraviantown), 38, *39*
Thompson, David, 41, *41*
Three Rivers, P.Q., 17, 18, 24, *25*, 26, 48
Thunder Bay, 80. *See also* Port Arthur.
Timmins, Ont., 80
Tlinkit Indians, 12
Tobacco Indians, 13
Tonti, Henri de, *21*
Toronto, Ont., 46, 48–49, 51
Tracy, Alexander de Prouville, Marquis de, *21*
Transportation, 78–81, *79*, *81*
   statistics, 93
Trent Canal, 65
Trois Rivières. *See* Three Rivers, P.Q.
Tsetsaut Indians, 12
Tsimshian Indians, 12
Tyendinaga Reserve, 36
Tyrrell, Joseph Burr, 68, 69

U

Ungava, District of, 67, *67*
Ungava Peninsula, *81*
United Nations, 84–85, *85*
United States, 33, *33*, 38–39, *38–39*, 43, *43*, 46–47, *47*, 56, *56*, 73–75, 82–83, *83*
   boundary settlements, 34–35, *34–35*, 40, *40*, 43, *43*, 53, *53*, 70, *70*
   fishing rights, 40, *40*, 54, *54*
Upper Canada, 37–39, 37–40, 46, 48, *49*, 51
Uranium City, 78, 80
Utrecht, Treaty of (1713), 22, *22*, 54, *54*

V

Valcour Island, 33
Valleyfield, P.Q., *99*
Vancouver, George, *41*, 41
Vancouver, B.C., 64, *64*
Vancouver Island, 43, *43*
Vergennes, Battle of, 39
Verrazano, Giovanni da, 4, 8, *9*, 11
Versailles, Treaty of (1783), 34, *34–35*, 54, *54*
Vespucci, Amerigo, 4, *7*
Victoria, B.C., 43
Viele, Arnout Cornelius, 20, *21*
Vignau, Nicholas, 16
Vikings, *3*
Vimy Ridge, 71, *71*
Vinland, 3, *3*

W

Wabana, Nfld., 77
Walcheren, Netherlands, 74–75, *75*
Waldseemüller, Martin, *7*
War of 1812, 38–39, *38–39*
Washington, George, 26, *33*
Washington, Treaty of (1871), 43, *43*
Waymouth, George, *15*
Webster-Ashburton Treaty (1842), 53, *53*
Welland Canal, 48, 51, 65
Welland Railway, 51
Wesel, Netherlands, 75
Westminster, Statute of (1931), 85
Whaling, *69*
Wheat, *60*
Whitehorse, Yukon, 70, 80, 82
White Pass, 70, *70*
William Henry (Sorel, P.Q.), 36, *36–37*
Windsor, N.S., 24
Windsor, Ont., 48, 51
Winnipeg, Man., 45, 56, *63*, 64, *64*
Winnipeg, Lake, *44*, 45, *62*, 62–63
Wolfe, Maj.-General James, *21*, 26–28, *27–28*
Wolseley, Garnet Joseph, Viscount, *56*, 62
Wolstenholme, N.W.T., *69*
Woods, Lake of the, 20, 21, 34, *34*, 40, *40*, 62, 62–63
World War, First, 71, *71*, 76
World War, Second, 72–76, *72–75*

Y

Yale, B.C., 43
Yellowknife, N.W.T., 78, 80
Yonge St., *51*
York, Upper Canada, 36, 46.
   See also Toronto.
York Fort, 20, 23, 31–32, 41, *44*, 45–46.
Ypres, Belgium, 71, *71*, 75
Yukon, District of, 67, *67*
Yukon River, 2, 70, *70*
Yukon Territory, 67, *67*
   gold rush, 70, *70*

Z

Zaltieri, Bolognino, *10*